Taking up pottery

Taking up pottery

Emmanuel Cooper

Arthur Barker Limited
5 Winsley Street London W1

33397

ISBN 0 213 99389 9

Printed in Great Britain by Bristol Typesetting Co Ltd
Barton Manor St Philips Bristol

Contents

List of Illustrations

Mary Rogers: stoneware bowls (*Council of Industrial Design Studio*)

Robin Welch: stoneware coffee set (*Nick Knowland*)

Carol Steward: white glazed stoneware box

Joanna Constantinidis: stoneware wavy pots (*Council of Industrial Design Studio*)

Hylton Nel and John Nowers: earthenware figures (*Ceramic Review*)

Hylton Nel and John Nowers: red earthenware bowl (*Ceramic Review*)

Introduction

Making pottery has recently become a very popular activity. Professional studio potters continue to increase in numbers and more and more homes are being equipped with a small pottery workshop. Little equipment, other than clay, is needed in the first place to discover just how quickly even unskilled hands can make attractive and useful objects. More advanced pottery, of course, is not made without more complicated equipment, though this need not daunt the non-technically minded.

In this book the totally unskilled beginner is led in easy stages through the collection and preparation of clay with all the possibilities of its use, to the setting up of a small workshop. The use of technical terms and unnecessary technical information have been avoided. Instead I have explained only those points which have a practical value and lead on to the next process.

Basic techniques which are covered in detail include the preparation of dug and bought clay, and comprehensive details of how pots can be made by hand, using pinching, coiling and slabbing techniques. A wide variety of moulded methods are described in detail; throwing pots on the potter's-wheel, perhaps the most difficult of the potter's making methods, is given an entire chapter and each step is fully explained. Glaze preparation and application are dealt with as are kilns and firing. Chapter 10 explains how a small workshop can be set up and organized and lists necessary equipment together with the names and addresses of suitable manufacturers and suppliers.

The difference between stoneware and earthenware pottery is clearly explained and the materials required for each are fully listed. All the making methods are suitable for both types of ware.

I have tried in this book to introduce the beginner to the basic techniques involved in making pottery and how they can be extended and adapted to individual requirements. Once basic processes have been acquired the craft becomes a marvellous tool for experiments of all sorts some of which I have tried to indicate. In the hands of the potter, clay becomes a versatile medium, and, when plastic, responds to immediate pressure. Our response, in return, can bring great delight and enjoyment as well as a quantity of useful and decorative objects which can, in both their making and using, enrich our lives. Have fun!

Emmanuel Cooper
London 1971

1

Clay: The Raw Material

Clay is a naturally occurring earth which, when soft, has the ability to be formed into a wide variety of shapes by many different techniques and, when hard, to retain that shape. The ability of clay to be squeezed and modelled without crumbling apart is known as its plasticity. The other significant quality clay has, apart from being plastic, is that when it is heated in a fire or a kiln to a temperature above red heat (about 600°C) it changes physically and chemically. Fired clay is no longer affected by water but is hard and strong. The higher the temperature, the tougher and less porous the clay becomes. When it has been fired, clay changes into pottery, and such pottery is known as biscuit ware. A further firing with a covering of glaze will give the pot a completely smooth and waterproof surface, which is how most pottery is finished. The home potter does not need large quantities of complicated equipment, only the basic material clay is essential at the beginning and that is the subject of this chapter.

Depending on the amount of water present in clay, it is a formless sticky mess, a liquid slurry or slip, plastic, leatherhard or dry. Clay can be worked in each state in different ways; plastic clay, for example, can be carved and as a slip it can be poured into hollow moulds and cast, which is how the majority of industrial pottery is made.

Pottery can be divided into different types according to the temperature at which it was fired.

EARTHENWARE Low temperature, unglazed pottery such as that made in parts of Africa today is one sort of earthenware. The majority of earthenware however is fired to about 1100°C and has a smooth glazed surface. The clay (usually known as the body of the pot) is slightly porous and the glaze remains as a distinct layer on the surface.

STONEWARE Pottery fired to between 1200°C – 1350°C is known as stoneware. At this temperature the body softens slightly and becomes hard, vitrified and non-porous, the glaze and body are fused slightly together. Some stoneware is glazed with salt which is introduced into the kiln at high temperature. This gives a thin characteristic 'mottled' or 'tiger-skin' glaze.

PORCELAIN True porcelain is fired to temperatures usually similar to, or above that of stoneware; it is white and translucent and is normally delicately made with thin walls. Fine, translucent pottery, sometimes known as soft-paste porcelain, or bone china, is made from a specially prepared body which contains a high proportion of bone ash or some other ingredient which causes the body to vitrify at around 1150°C. The glaze firing is usually at a lower temperature – about 1050°C.

It is important, when beginning to make pottery, to decide on the temperature at which you wish to work as early as possible. As a general rule, it is much better to explore fully a limited range of materials at one temperature, than it is to dabble with all the different sorts of pottery. Generally speaking earthenware offers greater scope for brighter colours and decoration while stoneware gives stronger and more functional bodies with more subdued colours. Porcelain is a fine ware which requires suitable materials, and is a technique best tried after stoneware has been learned. It is therefore outside the scope of this book. I would suggest that anyone without experience of pottery would be well advised to start by making earthenware and later stoneware. All the techniques described can be used for making ware fired to either temperature but each does need its own raw materials which are fully explained in Chapters 9 and 10.

Clay: where to obtain it

Digging your own

The simplest, cheapest and often most satisfactory source of clay for the small potter is that found or dug locally. In the country, farmers or anyone with a local knowledge of the countryside often know of deposits. Road works, streams, cemeteries are other possible sources. Clay can often be found and dug at a depth of about three feet. The general rules for its preparation and care are as follows.

1 Before collecting large amounts of clay test a small quantity first. Fire a small piece in the kiln to ensure it will withstand the temperature without bloating (forming large blisters). If the test is successful collect a large enough amount to use for some time – about one or two hundredweight.
2 Leave clay outside in a heap for the action of wind, rain and frost to improve its working qualities. A year is considered to be an ideal time, but most clays can be used after a few weeks.
3 Dry out clay completely, break into small lumps and soak in water for several days until a freely flowing slip is made. Stir regularly; stones will sink and twigs will float;

the slip can be put through a coarse 40 mesh sieve to remove all foreign bodies.

4 Allow clay to settle and pour or siphon off excess water. Put clay out to dry on a plaster drying block (explained on page 20).

5 Test clay fully. Most local clays fire only to earthenware temperature and their working qualities can often be improved by adding small quantities of sand (up to ten per cent) or fireclay (up to twenty per cent).

Buying clay

It may not be possible to dig your own clay, in which case it can be bought from pottery suppliers and usually ordered by post. Most catalogues list several types of clay and state that all are specially prepared and can be bought in plastic or powder form. Plastic clay is delivered almost ready for use but is relatively more expensive than the same clay in powder form which must be mixed with water and left for several weeks before it is in good working condition. Earthenware clay is usually listed as red or white. Red clay is the nicest to work with and contains iron oxide which gives its characteristic reddish-brown colour. Sometimes various clays are listed as containing grog. Grog is clay which has been fired and ground down to a coarse powder or grit. It is added to unfired clay to make it stronger and reduce the amount of shrinkage which takes place when the clay dries and is fired. White earthenware clays, often listed as modelling clays, are usually prepared for industrial use; they are very smooth and fine, are not easy to work and are best left until required for a specific purpose.

Stoneware clays are usually dark grey in colour in their raw state and again may be listed as grogged. All stoneware clays will fire at earthenware temperatures though earthenware clay will not withstand stoneware temperatures. Most stoneware clays fire a creamy-buff colour at 1250°C. Crank mixture and fireclay are sometimes included in the catalogues. Crank mixture is a high temperature plastic clay containing a large proportion of sand and grog and is useful for adding to bodies which are to be used for coiling or slabbing methods. Fireclay is a high temperature clay, usually dark grey in colour. It can be added to dug clay to improve its working qualities and to raise its firing temperature. When mixed with crank mixture it can be used for kiln furniture.

Clay quality

The working qualities of clay vary and each potter tends to adjust to the particular characteristics of his clay. However, most clays can be improved when their defects are recognized.

Short clays will crack and split easily during throwing – this is sometimes caused by excessive sand or fireclay; they are not over-plastic and will dry quickly without cracking.

Sticky clays usually have too much ball clay which retains water. They are usually good for throwing, but often have a tendency to crack when drying out especially if thick-walled, and are slow to dry out.

Plastic clay is one which will throw well, can be lifted off the wheel and will dry without distortion.

Lean clay is similar to short clay except that it is slightly more plastic.

Storage

Keeping plastic clay in a good workable condition ceased to be a major problem with the invention of polythene sheeting and bags. Any cupboard or space in which clay is to be stored, if lined with plastic, will further ensure the clay retains its water content. Lumps of clay of about 20lb tapped in neat blocks can be handled easily and if wrapped securely in polythene will retain moisture indefinitely. Masking tape or string will ensure that the sheeting does not come undone. Bins, preferably made out of plastic, can also be used for keeping clay in good working condition, and a sheet of polythene over a damp cloth will keep the clay moist. While working, clay can be kept moist by covering it with a damp cloth.

Preparing clay for use

Before being used, clay is prepared in three ways.

1 It must be checked for moisture content by rolling out a small piece between the hands and bending it. If it cracks, then more water is necessary. If the roll is sticky the clay may need drying out.
2 The clay must be made even throughout; hard and soft clay must be mixed completely in the process known as wedging.
3 Air bubbles must be removed as these prevent clay being worked smoothly. This process is called kneading.

Softening

Clay is softened by adding water. This can be done in a variety of ways.

1 Poke holes in a lump of clay. Fill these with water, cover with a damp cloth, wrap in polythene sheeting and leave for several days.
2 Knock clay into a block and cut into layers with a wire. Dip each layer into water, and bang the lump back together in the wedging process. Hard and soft clay and different sorts of clay can be mixed together by cutting them into slices, alternating the slices and banging them together.

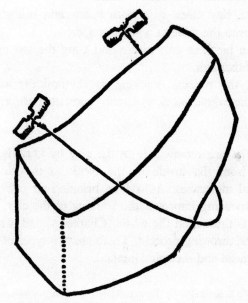

Figure 1 Cutting clay block before wedging

This process is known as layering.
Clay which is too soft can be covered with a dry cloth
and left to dry out slowly.

Wedging (figure 1)
Mixtures of hard and soft clay are banged together in the
process known as wedging by the following method.
1 Knock the clay into a brick shape. Large amounts can be
   handled by the experienced potter but beginners should
   try between 10–15 lb.
2 Work on a stout table which is not too high. Ideally the
   table top should be halfway between your knees and the
   tops of your thighs. A wooden surface is perhaps best
   though any surface will do.

B

3 Lift the clay block with both hands and bring it smartly down onto the table at a slight angle.
4 Cut the block in two pieces and bang the cut half on top of the other half.
5 Repeat the process, working as rhythmically as possible, until the whole block is evenly consistent throughout.

Kneading
Air bubbles are removed from the clay by kneading. Clay is brought from the inside of the block to the outside in a rhythmical movement. As well as bringing air bubbles to the surface, kneading improves the working of the clay, especially before it is thrown on the wheel (Chapter 5) and is an integral part of the throwing process. There are two types of kneading, the bulls head and the spiral method.

BULLS HEAD KNEADING (figure 2)
1 Knock a lump of clay of about 7lb into a brick shape.
2 Grasp the brick by both ends, palm of hands on upper corners.

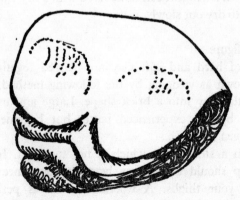

Figure 2 Bulls head kneading

3 Rock the block towards you, at the same time push slightly inwards, force the underneath upwards towards you and the whole block away from you.

4 Move your hands about two inches round the clay (anti-clockwise) and repeat the movement.

5 A bulls head will form when the technique has been mastered.

Figure 3 Spiral kneading

SPIRAL KNEADING (figure 3)

The advantage of this method is that larger amounts of clay can be dealt with and on the whole it is more effective.

1 Practice with a clay lump of about 7lb. As the name suggests this kneading is done by twisting the clay spirally in a clockwise direction.

2 Hold the clay with both hands. The right hand grasps the clay firmly and does more of the work. The left hand supports and guides the clay.

3 Lift the clay slightly and push the bottom half against the bench, twisting the whole lump slightly in a clockwise direction.

4 Move the hands round the clay and repeat the movement.

5 This technique needs plenty of practice and patience. Suc-

cess can be clearly seen when the clay takes on the appearance of a boxing glove. The clay must be pushed round without ever allowing it to overlap as this may trap in air. Clay can be sliced with a wire to check if all air bubbles have been removed and then knocked back together. Expert kneading however will make this unnecessary.

Figure 4 Wet clay

Clay reclaim (figure 4)

Clay which has been used and dried out can be reclaimed for use by first drying it thoroughly (unless the pieces are small), breaking it up into small pieces and soaking it in water for a day or two. Remove surplus water and put the slurry (which is how the clay is known at this stage) on plaster of Paris blocks to dry. Make the clay pat even and smooth and cover it with strong material. This helps the water to evaporate and prevents the formation of hard surface crust, as well as keeping the clay clean. When sufficiently hard, the clay can easily be lifted off the plaster, wedged and stored.

Stages of clay

Each clay stage is determined by the amount of water

present. The more water which is mixed with the clay the softer and more formless the clay seems; the less water present, the harder and less plastic the clay is.

Name	Description	Use
Slurry	Clay which is softened down in water until it is sloppy and formless. At this stage its use to the potter is very limited	Luting clay pieces together
Slip	Clay softened down in water until sloppy then put through a sieve (about 80 mesh) to give an even, smooth flowing liquid of a similar consistency to cream. Can be coloured by the addition of oxides. See page 102	Mainly used for decoration but is used on a large industrial scale for casting shapes in hollow moulds
Plastic	Clay which contains between twenty-five per cent and thirty per cent water and can be moulded and modelled into almost any shape in a wide variety of techniques. Does not stick to fingers, nor crack when bent	Ideal state for the majority of pottery processes
Leather or cheese hard	Contains enough water to allow clay slight movement. Cannot be bent far without cracking. Difficult to reclaim for use until allowed to dry out completely	Pots can be turned or carved. Slabs can be joined
Dry	Contains little or no physical water. Dry pots often appear lighter in colour at edges. Will break if attempts are made to bend it. Can be easily reclaimed by breaking into small lumps and soaking in water	Little can be made at this stage. Good stage for weighing out dry clay for slip or glaze recipes

Additions to clay

The working qualities of many clay bodies can often be improved by small additions of sand or grog and many clays can be given a different texture or colour to suit various purposes. It is wise to test small quantities first and to keep test bodies well away from the standard clay body.

SAND Almost any type of sand can be used: silver, beach (may need washing), builders, zircon, coarse or fine. Additions of more than ten per cent can sometimes make the body brittle. Small quantities often improve the working qualities of the clay, especially for throwing. It is very useful when added to bodies which are to be used for cooking pots – zircon sand is especially good.

GROG Many different grades of grog can be bought, ranging in size from dust to coarse. Fine grog strengthens bodies and often improves the throwing qualities. Coarse grog is unsuitable for throwing bodies but adds strength and texture to bodies for hand building methods.

IRON OXIDE Amounts up to eight per cent can be added to white or grey bodies to colour them brown, but at stoneware temperature such amounts may cause bubbles to form in the body, known as bloats, and distortion of the body.

MANGANESE OXIDE Amounts up to seven per cent can be added to colour the body black. At stoneware temperature such quantities would cause the body to bloat and probably collapse.

COBALT OXIDE Small amounts up to two per cent added to a white earthenware body will give a pale blue body.

IRON FILINGS Similar to iron oxide but will give speckled instead of even effect.

SAWDUST or CORK added to the clay will burn away in the firing to leave a textured body which, on certain pots, can be very successful. Experiment with different amounts first.

Quite pleasant when combined with iron filings.

ILLMENITE   A form of iron oxide which, when coarse, will speckle the body in a pleasant way.

Tools

Few tools are needed by the potter at the beginning. Only experience in handling clay will result in knowing when clay is too soft or too hard, and the hands are the only tools which will do this. When clay sticks to your fingers it is too wet, and when it forms itself into a compact lump and leaves your hands cleanly it may be just right. Before detailing the few tools needed, there are one or two points which can help in handling clay. Clay is, on the whole, a messy material. Even in the cleanest workshop a layer of dust seems to be continually settling from the fine clay particles. Protective clothing which completely covers ordinary clothes is more effective than an apron and should be removed when leaving the pottery.

The following tools are essential.

BENCH   A strong wooden table with stout legs makes a good working surface. A smaller, lower table, or a concrete shelf is ideal for wedging clay. The slightly absorbent surface which wood gives makes a pleasant working or wedging surface.

DRYING BLOCK   Reclaimed clay can be dried out in various ways. A bed of bricks, covered with a strong cloth, filled with reclaim clay which is covered over, will dry out the clay evenly if it is not too deep. Alternatively, clay can be put to dry on plaster of Paris blocks. The finished block should not be too heavy to handle and a good size is 16in x 16in x 3in. The blocks can be made by the following method.

1 Cardboard clothes boxes make good moulds in which to form the block. Alternatively the mould can be made up of four wooden walls on a smooth surface, such as perspex which is ideal as it is flexible, or glass. Put thin coils of clay round the edges of the wood to prevent plaster running out. Wooden surfaces need to be painted with soap solution to prevent plaster sticking to them.

2 Estimate amount of plaster required by calculating number of cubic inches. Approximately $2\frac{1}{2}$lb dry plaster in 1 quart of water = 80 cubic inches. Cubic inches = length x breadth x height.

Example, to make a block 16in x 16in x 3in = 768 cubic inches

therefore $768 \div 80 = 9\frac{1}{2}$ approximately

therefore $9\frac{1}{2}$ quarts water needed

and $9\frac{1}{2}$ x $2\frac{1}{2}$ = 24lb plaster approximately.

3 A mixture of $2\frac{1}{2}$lb of plaster of Paris in 1 quart of water gives a block of plaster which is fairly soft but very absorbent. A mixture of 3lb plaster in 1 quart of water gives a harder, but denser plaster block.

4 Ordinary builders' plaster is not suitable and potters' plaster of Paris should be bought from a supplier. When only small quantities are required use fine dental plaster, which can usually be bought at local chemists.

5 Sieve the plaster through a coarse sieve, such as a kitchen sieve, to break up any lumps.

6 Measure ingredients and gently sprinkle the plaster into the water (never add water to plaster). Leave to slake for three minutes.

7 Gently stir the water and plaster and mix thoroughly with your hand. Try to avoid stirring in air bubbles.

8 When the plaster begins to thicken, pour it into the pre-pared mould.

9 Allow to set for at least an hour before handling.

Tough fabric can be used to line the mould before pouring in the plaster. This prevents the plaster block being chipped in use and ensures that no plaster gets into the clay. Clay which is contaminated with plaster cannot be fired, as plaster can cause the pot to crack before or during the firing, and should be thrown away.

WIRE Strong wire is necessary to cut the clay. Nylon fishing line is strong but is not so pleasant to use as metal wire. Two or three strands twisted together gives a good strong wire. Fasten the ends on wooden toggles or washers but ensure that the wire tips are bent backwards from the centre so that when pulling with the wire the sharp ends do not cut into your fingers. To make a twisted wire, fasten a heavy weight to one end of the strands, support the other end, and spin the weight so causing the wire to twist.

SPONGES Two sorts of sponges are required. One should be large for wiping benches, and the other small and fine (natural sponges are ideal) for smoothing pots and for use when throwing pots.

SCRAPERS Benches need to be scraped occasionally to remove dry clay and paint scrapers are ideal for this. Never scrape plaster blocks to remove clay as this may scrape away some of the plaster. If the clay sticks, leave the block to dry out and the clay will come off easily.

STORAGE BINS Clay can be kept in good working condi-tion wrapped in polythene sheets or stored in a moisture-proof plastic bin or cupboard. Individual pots can be stored in biscuit tins or in a specially prepared airtight damp cupboard. Blocks of plaster soaked in water will help to keep the cupboard damp.

BOARDS Never work directly on the surface of the table but work on either tiles (unglazed side), boards or pieces of asbestos which are usually quite flat and can be broken easily into convenient sizes.

2

Exploration

Most people, as soon as they handle clay, want to rush immediately to the wheel and make superb coffee sets. Unfortunately, their lack of expertise is sufficient to convince them that they will never be able to make 'proper' pots. They forget that it takes up to five years to master the complex art of throwing which is, perhaps, the most skilled technique of the potter. There are numerous other equally interesting ways of working clay and this chapter leads the beginner through other methods which combine the making of useful objects with the gathering of maximum experience.

Tiles

Potters have for many hundreds of years made flat pieces of clay and used them, mainly for building purposes. The Romans made terra-cotta roof tiles, the English medieval potters made small tiles about 4in square for the floors of churches and abbeys and decorated them with simple designs inlayed with clay of contrasting colour. The Islamic potters made richly coloured tiles, some with relief decoration, and the jewel-like effects they achieved are still as brilliant today as when they were made three or four hundred years ago.

Apart from the relatively straightforward way tiles are

made, they offer enormous opportunity for decorative treatment. Some techniques will be included in this chapter but more will be found in Chapter 6 on Decoration, many of which can be carried out on tiles to great effect.

Tiles which are made for a specific use often need to fulfil various basic requirements. If, for example, the tiles are to be fixed permanently to a wall they will need a roughened back to give the cement a grip. If they are for serving food they must be smooth and regular, in which case the design may well be painted to give a flat surface rather than decorated with slip which will give an embossed surface. These practical considerations must be borne in mind when planning your work.

First exercise: experiments with slabs

1 Roll out two 3lb lumps of grogged clay to a thickness of $\frac{3}{8}$in – $\frac{1}{2}$in. Roll it out on thick paper or a heavy material such as deck-chair canvas to prevent it sticking to the table. Try to get the clay as flat as possible but surface irregularities are not important in this exercise. Incidentally, any air bubbles in the clay will show as blobs and indicate incorrect or insufficient kneading.

2 Cut one slab into strips about 1in wide. Now join these on the other slab in various ways. Weave them, corrugate them like waves, roll them into spirals, stand them on their edge and so on. The idea behind making this decorative freely shaped panel, is to experiment with clay and discover what it can be made to do.

3 If you want to keep the finished panel then the pieces must be joined to the base by luting. Surfaces to be joined need to be scratched with a knife or pin and painted with a slurry, which is a liquid mixture of clay and water. Press both surfaces firmly together and strengthen the join

by moulding in thin strips of clay at the edges.

4 Experience will show that certain combinations of shapes work better than others and ideas can be worked out initially on paper. Finished work must be allowed to dry out slowly to prevent cracking and warping as clay contracts when it dries.

Second exercise: jewellery

Make small pendants, earrings, cuff-links, belts and such like. Model them carefully and finely and relate the decoration to the scale and use of the object. Beads too can be made. Long thin beads, teeth-like pointed beads, round beads, square beads and so on can all be made. Remember that clay shrinks and this should be accounted for when making the holes. Holes can best be made with the pointed end of a compass or some similar tool when the clay is leather hard. The special way beads are glazed and fired is dealt with in Chapter 9.

Third exercise: flat tiles

Use grogged clay to reduce the amount of shrinkage and assist even drying. There are two methods of making flat slabs or tiles; they can be made by either rolling out clay like pastry, if only one or two are needed, or can be sliced from a block if many slabs are required.

ROLLING (figure 5)

1 Work on strong paper or material. This prevents clay sticking to the table top and enables the slabs to be handled easily.

2 With the palms of the hands press out the clay flat.

3 Roll from the centre outwards and turn the clay over and round to make rolling easier.

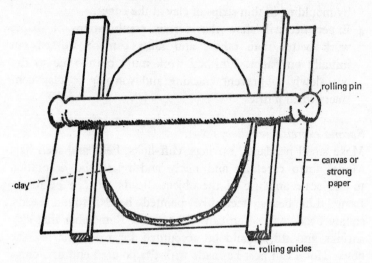

Figure 5 Preparing flat slabs of clay – rolling out method

4 To ensure even thickness, rolling guides can be used. These are wooden strips the thickness of the required tile, such as $\frac{7}{8}$in, $\frac{5}{8}$in or $\frac{3}{8}$in, which are laid either side of the clay and support the rolling pin.

5 The tile can best be cut to the required shape when it has hardened slightly; this prevents the cutting knife pulling it out of shape. Cut on the waste side of the clay, and use a wooden or metal rule to keep the cut straight.

6 Allow the tiles to dry out slowly. To prevent warpage stand the tiles on six layers of flat newspaper and cover with newspaper. Do not handle the tiles until quite dry.

7 Earthenware tiles can be fired in the kiln on stilts to prevent warping but stoneware tiles must be fired flat on the shelf as stoneware clay softens slightly in the firing.

LAYERING (figure 6)   Just as clay can be softened by being

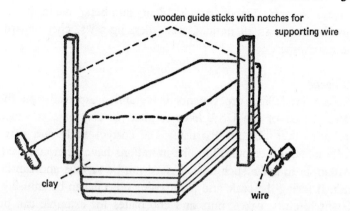

wooden guide sticks with notches for
supporting wire

clay

wire

Figure 6 Preparing flat slabs of clay – layering method

cut into thin slices and dipped in water, so it can be cut into flat, even tiles very quickly using the following method:

1 Knock prepared clay into an even block and stand it on a flat smooth surface. A marble slab is ideal.
2 Two wooden strips with saw marks at measured regular intervals, the width of the required tiles, are needed. Stretch a wire between the notches on the strips and, starting at the bottom of the block, push the wire through the block.
3 Move the wire to the next notch and repeat the process. Fairly soft clay is easiest to cut. The slabs need to be handled carefully to prevent warping. They can be stored if piled carefully on top of each other, separated by two or three sheets of newspaper and wrapped in plastic sheeting.

Tiles can be decorated in many ways, with clay added, carved, inlaid, painted, slip decorated, double-glazed and so on. The range is fully explained in Chapter 6 on decoration. Among the objects which can be made as tiles are bread and cheese servers, teapot stands, door numbers, name plates, house names, small notices, wall tiles, jig-saws, chess boards and dominoes.

Objects

Recent modelling experiments in ceramics especially on the West Coast of the USA have resulted in clay objects which imitate other objects. By using the correct scale and carefully matching colours, life-like imitations have been achieved. Attempts to make such objects need not be serious and can be fun. Altering the scale and juxtaposing objects can be amusing. Giant biscuits, cakes, nuts and chocolates for example can be imitated quite simply using slabs of clay; open packets of cigarettes or washing machines, furniture and so on need more patience and involve more modelling skill.

Murals

Once the skill of making and handling tiles has been achieved it is possible to plan and design a whole wall decoration. This can be carried out with separate tiles or designed as interlocking sections with joins at breaks in the design. Such a project needs detailed planning and the possibilities for decoration, colour and texture are almost endless. For anyone interested in pottery, making a mural is a fascinating means of combining the skill of the artist and craftsman.

First pots

A pot can be described as any clay form which acts as a container of some sort and the simplest way to make a pot is by shaping a bowl out of a ball of clay with your fingers. The method is straightforward in that few tools are required, but it is not quite as easy as it looks when done by an experienced potter. Clay has no 'natural' form; it takes on the form it is given provided the method of making the required form is within the working qualities of clay. There are a few useful guides which will help the beginner

1 Do not be impatient. Careful, rhythmical work will give greater success whichever technique you are using.
2 Prepare clay, grogged if preferred, slightly on the soft side.
3 Knock into round balls about 2in in diameter.
4 Have a small bowl of water handy in which to moisten your hands to prevent the surface of the clay drying.
5 Hold the clay in your left hand and press your right hand thumb down the centre of the ball until it is about $\frac{1}{4}$in from the bottom. Gently squeeze the clay between your thumb on the inside and your fingers on the outside, revolving the pot slowly in your left hand as you work. Press the clay with the flat part of your fingers rather than the ends, as these can easily make dents rather than force the clay upwards.
6 Keep the rim thick to prevent the pot spreading out into a shallow bowl. Aim first at pots in the shape of half a coconut (figure 7) though flatter bowls can also be made. The walls and base should be of equal thickness throughout and with experience this can be made very thin, almost $\frac{1}{8}$in.

Figure 7 Thumb pot

C

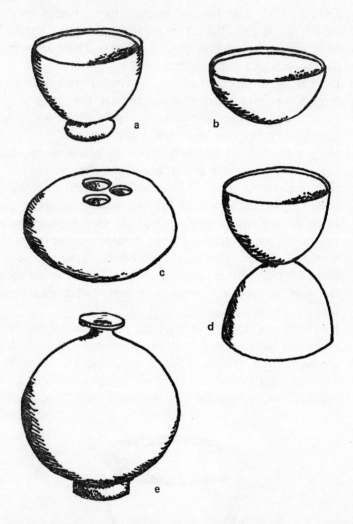

Figure 8 Thumb pots a Fitted coil foot b Flat thumb pot c Joined to form flower vase d Two joined thumb pots e Joined and fitted with foot ring and neck

7 To finish the pot, tap the bottom flat and, if necessary trim the top with a sharp knife or piece of wire.

Making thumb pots, as these small pots are sometimes called, is a useful way of discovering many of the working qualities of clay. For example, if you spend too long making them they will collapse as the clay gets 'tired'. If you wet your hands too much the clay will get soft and flop; if you allow the surface of the clay to dry out, it will become hard and crack when you squeeze it.

Many other forms can be made from small thumb pots (figure 8); for example pots of equal size can be joined together in a variety of ways. Dishes of the same size are made by using the same weight of clay. Such pots can be joined rim to rim, knocked into a stone shape and used as paper weights, though a small $\frac{1}{8}$in hole should be drilled to allow steam to escape from the inside when firing. Alternatively, a larger hole can be made in such forms for holding flowers. Two bowls can be joined using a balloon as a mould which can later be deflated or burst. The bowls can be joined base to base to make a dish on a stand. Several pots can be joined together to make an hors-d'oeuvre dish. Some bowls could be fitted with handles for cups. Coiled foot rings or small feet can also be added, and thumb pots are particularly useful for glaze tests.

3

Moulded Work

Any kind of support or pattern which is used to form a pot is known as a mould. It is highly probable that the first pots made by man were formed by smearing clay in either a basket or bird's nest, a hole in the ground or some similar hollow form. Because clay has no 'natural' form it is often made in the likeness of other more costly materials such as leather and metal, or pottery shapes are often copied directly from such natural objects as eggs, gourds, stones and shells. One of the quickest ways of making pots is to smear or wrap clay round or inside some sort of form or mould and in this chapter the use of moulds and the great extent of their use to the potter is explained.

Generally speaking, moulds are used for making those shapes which cannot be made easily or more quickly on the potter's wheel (Chapter 5). So round shapes are not usually moulded but thrown, though there is no technical reason why such shapes cannot be made in a mould if no wheel is available.

Ready made moulds

Almost any shallow shape can be used either as a hollow or a hump mould, for, in the widest sense, moulds are anything which can be used for forming shapes. Bowls and plates, provided they are smooth and rounded, can be used, though they usually have surfaces which are unsuitable. Clay sticks very easily to smooth, non-absorbent surfaces and this must be prevented. Flint of talc dusted on the surface of such moulds should prevent the clay from sticking. Stones, melons, coconuts and other natural forms can be used as hump moulds though their use is limited.

Cardboard boxes too, can be used for moulds. Cigarette boxes, washing-powder boxes and so on can all be used, though clay usually has to be pressed onto them and smeared round in the inside. Cardboard boxes tend not to make even, regular shaped pots, but are a mould form worth exploring.

Simple moulds

The simplest, quickest and easiest moulded pottery is made using flat slabs or tiles of clay (made by either the rolling or layering method explained on pages 29-31) laid inside a hollow container of some sort. The slabs must not be so thin that they will warp and be too weak when dry, nor be too thick to be formed in the mould. ⅜in or ⅝in thickness should be suitable for pots up to 12in wide.

Wooden stick mould (figure 9)

This is a very quick and effective method of making dishes.

1 On a paper or cloth lay out four sticks about ½in or ¾in thickness to form a square (figure 9a).
2 Roll out a slab of medium soft clay and cut to size required.
3 Lay the clay slab over the sticks and gently press clay into the centre to form a dish (figures 9b and c).

One variation of this simple method is to use fewer or more

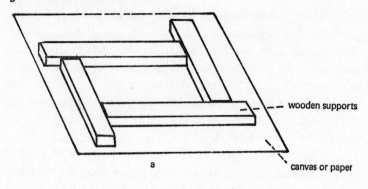

wooden supports

canvas or paper

a

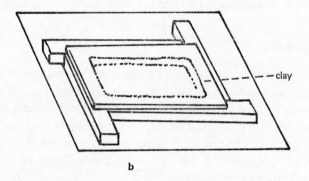

clay

b

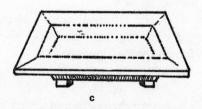

c

Figure 9 Method of making simple wooden stick mould   a Wooden
supports   b Filled with clay   c Finished dish with added feet

sticks to make three, five or six sided dishes. The thickness of the sticks should relate to the size of the dish, experience will determine what thickness is most suitable. Grogged clay should be used to make dishes over 6in in one direction, though of course it can be used for smaller ones. The edges of the dish need to be either cut cleanly and left crisp, or smoothed over with a fine sponge to make them round. Alternatively, a simple design can be impressed with a decorating tool. Slabs of clay which have been decorated with slip designs (pages 101-7) can be used for this mould.

Hammock mould (figure 10)
Canvas or other strong material suspended from the four legs

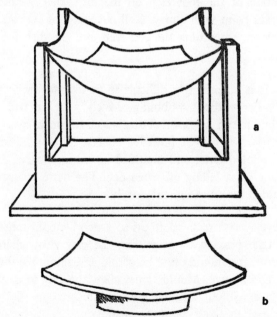

Figure 10 a Hammock mould b Pot made in hammock mould with added feet

of an inverted table or over the top of a large bowl will act as a mould to form pleasantly curved, rather shallow dishes (figure 10a). If the material hangs too loosely, the central dip will be too steep for the clay which may crease when put into the mould. Cut the clay slabs into shape before laying them inside the mould; they can be cut round, square, rectangular, television shaped and so on. Keep the edges neat.

Flat dishes are often improved by having feet fixed underneath (figure 10b). There are two different types and they are fixed on the pot when it has become leather-hard.

FOOT RINGS These can either be straight sided or round according to the shape of the dish. Measure and mark carefully the position of the foot ring on the dish, then scratch with a knife and paint with slurry. Roll out a coil of clay and press into position, smoothing the coil well into the dish for a firm join.

FEET It is surprisingly difficult to fit four feet which stand perfectly flat without wobbling. Much patience will be required but it can be done. Three feet are much easier to fix as they will not wobble however uneven they are. Feet must always be luted onto, and moulded into, the body of the dish to prevent them falling off when dry. The more securely they are moulded the more satisfactory they are.

Because clay contracts as it dries, a good mould must allow this to take place without pulling the clay. Any changes of direction in the mould must be gentle and smooth rather than angular and abrupt. Moulds must allow the clay to move over the surface without sticking and for this reason slightly absorbent moulds such as those made out of plaster-of-Paris or biscuit fired clay (known as pitcher moulds) are the best

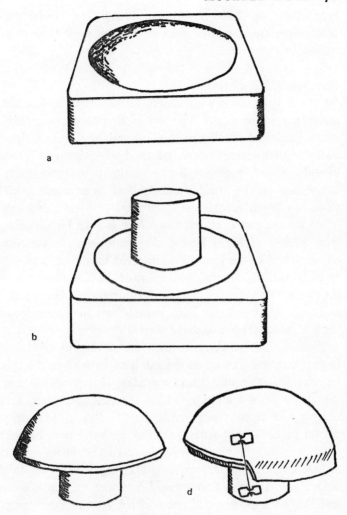

Figure 11 Making and covering a mushroom hump mould   a Plaster of Paris hollow mould   b Cast taken of plaster mould with stem added
c Finished mould with bevelled edge   d Trimming clay placed over mould

type. Metal or glazed moulds are difficult but can be used if first dusted with ground flint or talc to enable the clay to slide over the surface.

Hump moulds

So far I have dealt with simple hollow moulds, but simple hump moulds in which the clay is draped over moulds are also a quick and effective method for making dishes (figure 11). Balloons, for example, can be used as quick and versatile moulds. Wood, perhaps, is one of the pleasantest materials to use but wooden moulds usually have to be made specially. Rounded hump moulds are the easiest to handle and can be made for the purpose from clay which is then biscuit fired, or from plaster of Paris. Round clay hump moulds are thrown on the wheel in the form of an inverted mushroom and subsequently turned. Hump moulds made out of clay can only be made when proficiency as a thrower has been attained and therefore plaster of Paris moulds cast in a manufactured form of some sort can be made as an alternative.

Plaster of Paris hump moulds are similar to clay moulds in that they are mushroom shaped. This is to allow the clay to be trimmed off neatly round the edge. Hump moulds can be cast from hollow moulds, which are described later in the chapter, or from ready made round dishes. The original plaster mould of any surface on which plaster is to be poured must, however, be painted with several layers of soap solution to prevent the plaster sticking, allowing each layer to dry before applying the next layer. When the surface is smooth and shiny the plaster will not stick. A foot or stem must be cast onto the mould so that it will stand upright and enable the clay slab to be trimmed round the edge. The easiest way to make the stem is to cast the hump part and, before the plaster has set, push into it a cardboard tube and fill this with plaster. The plaster in the hump and stem will therefore join firmly together.

Clay slabs for hump moulds are prepared by either rolling out or by slicing. They are draped over the mould and are gently pressed into position with the palms of the hands to compress the clay to fit tightly round the mould. The danger of hump moulds is that, unless they are very shallow, they may prevent the clay from contracting and instead cause it to crack. Therefore only shallow dishes can be made successfully by this method. Feet or a foot ring can be moulded onto the base when it has hardened.

Making hollow moulds

However enjoyable and convenient it is to use moulds which already exist, there will come a time when moulds are required for a particular purpose. To begin with, the sort of mould you need will be determined by the way you intend to fill it with clay. There are basically two sorts of moulds, for two different techniques – the press-in and the casting types. There is not space in this book to go into the complex nature of how cast moulds are made or filled with a special sort of liquid clay; suffice it to say they are complicated and demand considerable knowledge of mould making and clay chemistry which the beginner would do well to leave until more experience has been gained.

Press-in moulds as the name suggests, are filled with either soft pieces or slabs of clay pressed into a hollow mould.

One-piece press-in moulds for clay slabs (figure 12)
Shallow dishes of any size between 3in to 12in wide can be made very well by this method. These moulds do have one or

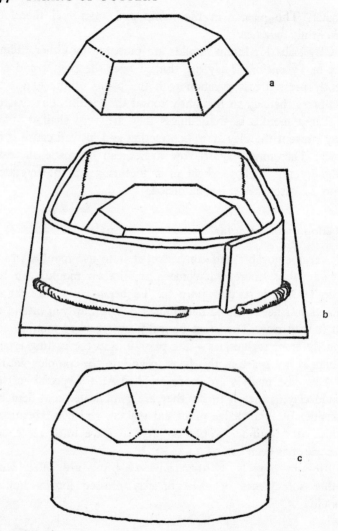

Figure 12 Making a moulded dish a Solid form of dish b Arrangement for casting solid dish in plaster c Cast mould with solid clay removed

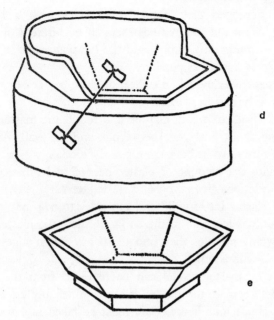

Figure 12   d Filling the mould   e Finished pot with added foot ring

two limitations.

1 The shape has to be designed to allow the pot to contract freely within the mould, therefore a foot of any sort cannot be included in the design.

2 The dish cannot be more than 12in wide nor 3in deep, nor less than 3in wide or ¾in deep as outside these limits the amount of clay is difficult to handle successfully.

3 Sharp changes of direction must be avoided. It is difficult to get clay in the angles and they tend to hold the clay back and prevent even shrinkage.

METHOD OF MAKING MOULD

1 Make original solid master, in shape of finished pot, from

fine ungrogged clay. Smooth the sides with a hacksaw blade. With the serrated edge scratch in different directions to cut through any bumps and use the plain edge to get the surface as smooth as possible.

2 Put the master model on a sheet of glass, perspex or asbestos ready to be cast in plaster.

3 Build a wall of wood, clay or lino round the master model leaving about ¾in space between it and the wall. Allow an extra 1½in of wall above the top of the model.

4 Estimate the amount of plaster needed and mix according to instructions given on page 24, Chapter 1.

5 Pour plaster into mould and tap sides to help any trapped air bubbles to come to the surface. Allow the plaster to set for twenty minutes then smooth off any rough edges on the corners with a knife.

6 The clay master model can be removed from the plaster cast as soon as the plaster has set sufficiently hard which takes about four hours. Care must be taken not to damage the plaster mould.

7 Allow the mould to dry out slowly before use; rapid drying by heating will ruin the plaster and the mould.

FILLING THE MOULD The thickness of the clay slab will depend on the size of the mould. Rolling out clay on canvas helps when handling the slab if the mould is large. Coarser materials such as hessian give deeper textures which may or may not be desirable.

1 Place the slab of clay into mould and roughly trim off any surplus though leave ½in spare at edge.

2 Ease and press the clay into all parts of the mould. When the mould is completely filled, trim the edges with a wire resting on top of the mould held at right angles and horizontal to the edge.

3 The rim can either be cut sharp or left crisp, impressed with a wooden tool pattern or sponged smooth and round.

Simple one-piece moulded dishes can be used for a wide variety of purposes. Fitted with feet they make elegant and practical serving dishes for fruit or vegetables. Using a suitably prepared clay they can be used as cooking dishes; when glazed only on the inside they can be very handsome, especially when red clay has been used. Moulded dishes can also be joined together to make sculptural forms and can form the basis for a whole series of successful and original pots.

Two or more piece moulds
Complex forms and lidded pots can be made in moulds which have two or more pieces. This allows complex shapes to be made in a mould which is taken off the pot piece by piece. I would recommend that the beginner attempts a two-piece mould before making more complex ones which require more pieces.

Box moulds (figure 13)
One of the most useful and successful press moulds is the box mould. Small, lidded ceramic boxes can be extremely attractive and afford plenty of opportunity for all aspects of design as well as being ideally suited to this method of manufacture.

METHOD OF MAKING MOULD
1 Decide on the shape and size of the box; sketches are often a great help in working out accurately the most suitable proportions.
2 Make a solid master shape of the complete box in fine clay. Ensure there is no undercutting which would prevent the

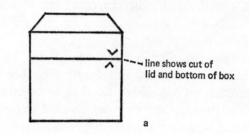

line shows cut of
lid and bottom of box

a

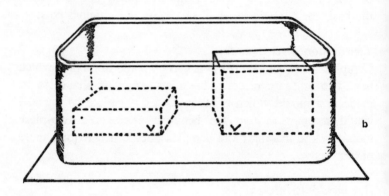

b

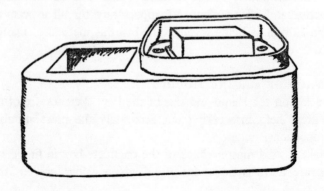

c

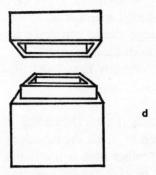

Figure 13 Making a box mould   a Solid form of box   b Arrangement for casting lid and bottom half of box in plaster of Paris   c Plaster mould of box showing arrangement for casting plaster of Paris mould for lid flange   d Finished box showing lid flange

finished box sliding out of the mould. Smooth the sides of the master by burnishing if necessary.

3 Cut off the top part of the master which is to form the lid.

4 Stand both parts, bottom (upside down) and lid of box on a sheet of glass or perspex and build wall round, ready for casting the two halves in a single mould. Leave about 2in space between the two parts.

5 Cast in plaster and leave to set for four hours.

6 To make the mould for the lid flange, model a central clay block on the bottom half of the box while it is still in position inside the mould. The block has to allow the thickness of the wall of the lid round it.

7 Make three suitable key holes with a small coin on the mould on the bottom half of the box and paint the plaster with several layers of soap solution, allowing each to dry before applying the next layer.

D

8 Build a clay wall on top of the mould round the block in which to cast the flange mould.

9 Cast the flange mould and leave the plaster to set before removing it from the base mould.

10 Remove master clay model and allow mould to dry slowly before using it.

FILLING THE MOULD Depending on the size of the box you have chosen to make, the moulds are best filled by smearing clay inside rather than trying to put it in as slabs, though strips or coils of clay can be used and will leave a pleasant pattern on the outside.

SMEAR METHOD
1 Prepare clay slightly softer than usual, grogged if preferred.

2 Estimate the amount of clay required to fill the bottom half, make it into a ball, press it into base and smear it up the sides. Make sure it goes into all corners, and the walls are evenly thick throughout. The thickness can be tested with a pin or needle stuck in the end of a cork.

3 Place flange mould into position and add extra clay on the inside, moulding it securely onto the base to form the flange of the box.

4 Fill the lid part of the box, making sure edges are crisp and neat and the thickness of the wall is the same as that allowed by the flange on the bottom half of the box.

5 Remove top and bottom halves of the box when leather-hard from the mould and fit together, trimming flange if necessary.

When handling moulds care must be taken not to damage them, or get plaster of Paris in the clay. You will find your fingers are the most sensitive tools to use, though wooden tools are useful for smoothing surfaces. Over-sponging the surface of the box will tend to roughen it rather than make it smooth and may also cause the clay to warp if it gets unevenly wet.

I have described how to make a simple box pressed mould. Once the idea of press moulding is understood, more complex forms can be made. When filling the mould, follow the general principle that the inside profile should follow the outside profile. The technique can be extended to using different moulds to make different parts of the pot which are joined together when leather hard. Even the complex form of a teapot can be made by this technique.

Wrap-round pots

So far in this chapter I have dealt with aspects of moulds, mould making and the use of slabs and pressed clay. There is one other variation which will follow well here, and that is the 'wrap round' pot. Simply, clay slabs are wrapped round a central mould which must be removed before the clay contracts. It is a quick and effective method of making either decorative or functional pots, based on a cylinder (figure 14).

1 Prepare clay slabs by the rolling out or layering method.
2 Cover mould with newspaper loosely held in place with Sellotape. The paper will prevent the clay sticking to the mould which can then be removed easily without damaging the pot.
3 Stand mould on prepared base of clay, and wrap slab round mould, welding it firmly to the vase, using a thin layer of slip if necessary. The side join can either be smoothed over or incorporated as a feature of the design of the pot.

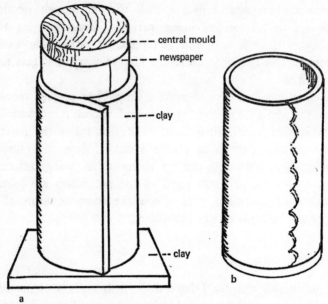

Figure 14 Wrap-round pot a Central mould b Finished pot with join incorporated as feature of design

4 Remove the mould as soon as the walls will support themselves without sagging. The newspaper can then be removed easily. Any which is stuck will burn away in the kiln.

Suitable moulds are such things as pieces of scaffolding, rolling pins, bricks and tins; in fact any shape which can be removed without damaging the pot. Clay slabs must relate in thickness to the size and purpose of the pot; coffee cups, for example, would need to be reasonably fine, thin and rounded at the edge.

There are certain types of expanded polystyrene which though firm and solid are light and burn completely away when exposed to flame. Such material can be used as internal moulds for shapes which do not allow the mould to be removed. The polystyrene must, however, be removed before the pot contracts and this can be done very quickly by applying a flame from a Bunsen burner or blow lamp.

Decorating slabs

Slabs for wrap round pots can be decorated in a number of ways before being used. Rolling them over textured or decorated surfaces is a quick and effective method. A plaster block can, for example, be cast from a decorated clay slab, and, providing the decoration is not too detailed, the clay, rolled over the block, will take on the pattern. Even textured surfaces, made by rolling clay over such things as coarse material or hardboard, can be successful, as can the more uneven textures obtained from, for example, compressed cork or other similar open composite building materials. Slabs rolled over thin twigs or leaves take on their attractive pattern which can form the basis of rich designs.

4

Hand Built Forms

The technique of building pots without using a mould of some sort dates back to neolithic times and is still practised by natives in different parts of the world today. There are basically two techniques, one is to build coils or rings of clay on top of each other, and the other is to join slabs of clay together in a sophisticated form of ceramic carpentry. There are several advantages of building pots by these methods; the shape is not limited by any mould nor, in the case of throwing, by the centrifugal force which makes all pots round; pots of almost any size can be made; for example in West Africa, grain storage pots are made 9ft tall. Lastly, and perhaps most important, the form of the pot evolves slowly and can be considered at all stages.

Coil pots

There are many variations on the basic technique of building up the walls of a pot by joining pieces of clay together. Some potters use round coils, other flat coils, some use odd pieces and some use strips. Whichever method is used, all the pieces have to be smoothed together to form a solid wall. Separate coils or pieces should not be left as such but must be moulded firmly into each other to give the pot mechanical strength. Occasionally one sees coil pots in which all the coils are left quite separate and distinct: such a pot is mechanically very weak. Joining the coils together need not necessarily mean that the surface should be completely smooth and flat; coils can be joined together in a way that gives rise to a rhythmical pattern which can give a pleasant and rich texture.

The shape and size of coil pots have a range which is almost limitless, the only practical limit, apart from the kiln facilities and so on, is that of suitability. For example, it is probably more expedient to use slabs rather than coils to make a square shaped pot, just as small pots can best be made as thumb pots. The coiling technique is very versatile being easily adapted for many uses. The potter Rosemary Wren builds animals using rings of clay, adapting and simplifying the animal form to the technique.

For the beginner it is best to gain experience by following a straightforward coiling method which can be adapted to suit personal requirements as experience is gained.

1 Prepare clay medium soft, grogged if the pot is to be very large.

2 Make base by knocking out clay into a flat slab and cut to required shape. The first coil always goes directly at the edge on top of the base.

3 To make coils, squeeze clay into thick sausages, and, on a clean area of the table, roll into long coils using the full length of your hands. This will help to prevent the clay from forming an oval shaped section. With experience it will be no problem to make coils over 3ft long. Some African potters make coils by rolling the clay vertically between their hands which is a method you may like to try. The thickness of the coil will rarely need to be more than half an inch depending on the size of the pot and the

exact method of working. Before fixing the coils to the pot you can slightly flatten them by pressing them with your fingers.

4 Flatten the ends of coils to ensure that no air is trapped inside and place first coil in position on top edge of base. Press side of coil on base both on the inside and outside.

5 Fix second coil on one below before adding next coil. To make the pot go outwards fix coil on outer edge of lower coil; to make pot go inwards fit coil to inner edge of lower coil.

6 The wall can be made thinner by beating it with a wooden spoon. Support the walls on the inside with your hand or wood in the shape of a mushroom and tap the outside wall upwards. This not only makes the wall thinner and also taller, but it knocks the coils together to form a stronger bond. This method of pot building, known as the paddle and anvil technique, dates back some 2,000 years to the Indus Valley and is still used, among other places, in parts of India and Africa.

7 The shape of the pot needs to be considered carefully as it gets bigger. A banding wheel which enables the pot to be turned as it is made, makes the whole process of building and consideration much easier. It may be found necessary to allow the bottom half of the pot to harden slightly before the top half can be built, in which case, the lower rim must be kept soft. This can be done by temporarily covering it in silver foil which provides a tight close fit and is quick to apply. When the top of the pot is narrow a weighted stick, such as a pestle, can be used to tap the inside out slightly and correct any unwanted hollows in the wall. African potters trim and shape their pots as they work; any small pieces of clay which are removed are put back to fill any slight hollows or depressions.

8 Unevenness on the rim can be trimmed using a needle in the end of a cork or with a wire. Regular trimming will help your pot to come up evenly.

9 Once the coils have been pressed and moulded firmly together, both on the inside and the outside, the mechanical requirements have been fulfilled. There are various ways of smoothing the outside if this is preferred. Initially this is done with the fingers and later with a wooden tool of some sort. When the pot is leather hard it can be smoothed further by using a hacksaw blade. The serrated edge, scratched in all directions, will cut through all the small irregularities and the plain edge can be used for the final smoothing. Burnishing is another smoothing technique in which the surface of the leather-hard clay is rubbed, or burnished, with a hard smooth tool such as a pebble or a wooden modelling tool. Red clays burnish more easily than other clays and, when fired, are a pleasant coral colour. Grey and white clays can be more easily burnished by first rubbing on dry iron oxide, though this will stain the finished pot.

Coiling and throwing

Once the wheel had been invented, the technique developed of coiling rings of clay onto pots and then smoothing the the walls by throwing on the wheel. This technique is specially useful for making large pots. There are basically two ways in which large pots can be made: one method is to throw the pot in sections and join them together when they have stiffened; the other is to build the pot up with coils and about every 3 or 4in throw the wall up. Some skill in throwing is required and the technique is an advanced one though not outside the scope of the home potter.

1 Make base of pot by coiling, throwing or moulding.

2 Set base in centre of wheel. A kick wheel is best as it gives the greatest control but an electric wheel or banding wheel can be used. Secure base of pot to wheel head using rolls of clay.

3 Use softer clay than usual, add coils by normal method and mould in as smooth as possible. Add three or four coils before throwing.

4 There are a number of ways of throwing coils. Some potters use fingers, some wooden tools, though I prefer a combination of both. Get the wheel moving at medium speed, moisten your hands and using your forefingers bent round to give a good grip, throw the clay up. Sufficient water must be used to allow free movement of the clay without dragging, but water must not be allowed to trickle down the pot as it may cause a split.

5 A wooden tool or wooden rib held on the outside wall at an angle of 45° will help to smooth, as well as throw, the pot.

6 To make the shape go inwards or outwards the coils must be put on the inner and outer edges respectively. Before any major changes in direction are made, the soft walls must be allowed to harden slightly or the coiling and throwing process may easily distort the shape.

Coiled pots need not be made round though it will be found that round pots are the quickest pots to make by coiling. The technique of coiling and throwing will only allow round pots to be made.

Pots to make

Coil pots do not necessarily have to imitate the smooth regular qualities of wheel-thrown pots, though they can be made so that they do. Slight unevenness and irregularity often comes as a result of coiling and these qualities can be incorporated into the sort of pottery made and can often enhance it. Lamp bases or flower vases are good examples of pots which do not necessarily have to be symmetrical. Garden pots, plant pots and plant pot holders, bread bins, flour bins, candlesticks, serving dishes and cider jars, stools, low chairs and small tables are other examples which can be made by coiling or coiling and throwing.

Slab pots

In Chapter 3 I dealt in some detail with how to make slabs and how to use them for moulded dishes and wrap-round pots. Clay slabs can be used, however, without a mould and can be built into functional or decorative objects. Slabs can be left flat and joined together to make straight-sided pots with clean sharp corners, or they can be bent and fitted together to form undulating pots with all the softness and subtlety the skill of the potter can achieve. The following working notes on the technique may be helpful to the beginner.

1 Grogged clay is more able to withstand the stresses of slab work. The slab can either be rolled or sliced.

2 The thickness of the slabs will depend on size of the pot but $\frac{3}{8}$in thickness would be average for most pots.

3 Allow slabs to stiffen slightly before use. This is best done by laying them on several sheets of perfectly flat newspaper.

4 Calculate measurements before starting to cut slabs, and work to a template to avoid mistakes. A wooden or metal cutting guide held on the piece required is almost essential. Use a thin sharp knife, and cut with several light cuts rather than one heavy one. Always rest the walls of the pot on top of the base and calculate accordingly.

5 Joints can be carried out in several ways. They can be cut at right angles and butted together which is probably the simplest, or cut at angles of 45° which is more difficult but is often the neatest.

6 Slabs which are to be joined together must be in the same state of hardness. If two slabs of different hardness are joined together they will be quite likely to split apart when drying. All joins must be luted firmly together and each surface firmly pushed together to give them a good grip. The inside of the join should be strengthened by moulding in a thin coil of clay. Where this cannot be done by the fingers a wooden tool should be used. In tall pots, the base or top should not be added until the joins are welded firmly together on the inside.

7 Large walls can be supported in the initial stages by bricks or buttresses of clay. On the inside of pots strips of paper screwed into a ball can also be used to prevent the walls sagging inwards. Thin strips of paper are easier to

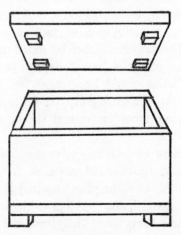

Figure 15 Slab box showing arrangement of slabs on base, with added feet

remove than crumpled paper, though they can, if necessary, be left to burn away in the kiln.

8 The nature of the slab pot will be determined to a large extent by the treatment of the corners. Sharp angular clean corners, for instance, only remain so when treated carefully. For example, when joining two walls, support one wall with a board rather than your fingers or hand which may well cause dents and ridges. Alternatively the corners can be smoothed round and the whole nature of the pot changed. The only useful advice is to treat all the corners in the same way. Corners can be sharpened when the pot has become leather-hard by using a hacksaw blade.

Boxes

In Chapter 3 I explained how to make box moulds for small boxes; another way of making boxes is to use clay slabs. These boxes have a different character to those made in a mould (figure 15). It is best to work from a template cut from card or stiff paper and, initially, not attempt boxes which are too large. Lids can be held in place by either a flange or by corner stops placed underneath. Knobs or handles are not functionally required on those lids which can comfortably be held in the hand. Rectangular butter dishes which hold a full half pound of butter are an obviously useful item which can be made by this method. So are rectangular flower holders which have holes pierced in the top to hold the flowers. Alternatively the top can be latticed with strips of clay interwoven to leave holes for the flowers.

Once the skill of handling clay slabs has been mastered, then the joy of experimenting with the technique and discovering its possibilities can be explored. Many-sided boxes can be made, though the angle at which they join must be calculated and cut accurately. Large flat slab pots can be made by building the narrow sides onto a large side, then carefully rolling the last one into position, luting coils into the joins as it is rolled along.

Earlier I mentioned that slabs need not be left flat and fascinating pots can be made using curved clay. It is difficult to bend slabs once they have begun to stiffen as they are quite likely to crack apart and once a slab has cracked it is almost impossible to close it up with any success. To curve slabs, lay them in slings or hammocks or drape them over suitable formers which can be improvised from rolling pins or tins. These slabs are handled the same way as flat slabs, and a wide variety of decorative forms can be made by this method.

Slabs can be made into lampshades, garden pots, bread bins, jars, vases, tea caddies, cheese dishes, flat serving dishes, toast racks and so on. I have even heard of one student making a slab built coffee set. There seems to be no limit once the technique has been mastered.

Slab built toys

The ancient Egyptians were among the first people to make toys out of clay. Many can be made from slabs in one form or another.

MAZES Simple or complex mazes date back several thousands of years and miniature ones can be made out of clay slabs built on a tile. The walls are luted firmly into position but care is needed so that the finished results are not messy. Lids can be made and in fact the complexity of the maze need not be limited to that which can be obtained on a flat surface. Boxes, fitting inside other boxes, for example, would be a challenge to design as well as to make.

HOUSES AND BUILDINGS   Children love to play with minia-
tures of objects which are important to them. The success of
the dolls' house, garage, fort, theatre, speed track, farm and
so on, cannot be denied. All of these can be made out of clay.
Whole villages of houses complete with school, church and
cinema have been made and provide an interesting challenge
for the potter as well as a pleasing toy for the recipient.
Modelled figures can also be made to use in the toys; these
could be cut out of slabs of clay or modelled in three dimen-
sions.

Working models can also be made in the form of human
or animal figures, farm carts with wheels, caravans, cars,
buses and so on. The skills that are required are those of the
potter and the engineer but the pleasure from such work
can come both in the making and the using of the objects.

5

Working on the Wheel

Anyone who has watched a skilled potter at work on a potter's wheel cannot fail to find it an impressive sight. In the hands of the potter the clay appears to have a life of its own, going up into a cone, down into a mushroom and eventually forming a tall cylinder, or a wide bowl or a narrow necked bottle.

Making pots on the wheel is a difficult technique which is only learned by patience and constant and regular practice. To say otherwise would be to give a false impression. This chapter covers all the basic steps of throwing and wheelwork and the steps are best taken one at a time. Any attempt to take in all the steps at once can only result in disappointment. There are no short cuts when learning to throw and regular daily practice is ideal. These notes will, I hope, help the beginner to overcome many difficulties and to avoid many mistakes encountered with throwing. All the necessary fundamental moves are explained step by step.

Clay preparation
Clay must be carefully prepared before starting to work. Badly prepared clay will defeat even the most experienced potters.
1 It must be thoroughly wedged and kneaded before being used. Prepared clay kept overnight must be kneaded again before use.

Emmanuel Cooper: stoneware breadcrock, dolomite glaze eighteen inches high. Made by throwing and coiling method

Right:
Sheila Fournier:
stoneware bowl nine
inches across. Made
by using throwing,
pinching and coiling
techniques. This bowl
successfully combines
form and decoration

Geoffrey Swindell:
stoneware forms. The
biggest pot is four
inches high. Press-
moulded forms are
joined together and
worked by squeezing,
pinching and coiling

Marianne de Trey:
two stoneware pots.
Wheel thrown, beaten
square and carved

Right: Mary Rogers:
stoneware lidded pot
four inches in dia-
meter. Subtle
combination of simple
forms with carved
decoration

Emmanuel Cooper: stoneware box three inches high. Made by the method described on page 47, this box is decorated with a simple geometrical painted slip pattern

Below: Michael Casson: stoneware pot nine inches high. A thrown pot, decorated with the paper resist technique using red and white slip. Landscape is the basis of this sensitive decoration

David Vaughan: pencil forms, earthenware. Here, clay has been used for forms other than pots. The results can be startling and successful

Ian Godfrey: stoneware pot. Little drawers decorated with symbols and patterns and house shapes based on those from the Far East, give this work an exotic and toy-like charm

Eileen Lewenstein: flower holder four inches high. Using a square press-moulded pot for the base, the top has been added with a lattice-like effect. The sculptural qualities of the pot are brought out by the dry textured glaze

Eric James Mellon: stoneware bowl ten-and-a half inches in diameter. Different glazes have been used to decorate this bowl with the circus horse and rider. Colour, texture and design have been used creatively and after many careful tests with different sorts of ash glaze

Below: Mary Rogers: two stoneware bowls about three-and-a-quarter inches high. A combination of coiling, pinching and scraping techniques have been used to build these finely made small bowls

Robin Welch: stoneware coffee set with a wood-ash glaze. Unity of design has been achieved by a subtle use of a basic straight-sided cylindrical form for most of the shapes. Well placed handles and spout give a functional quality. Areas of unglazed body give a pleasant contrast with the glaze

Carol Steward: stoneware lidded box about three inches high. A white dolomite glaze has been used over a grogged stoneware body. The carved lid gives this little box an admirable sculptural and tactile quality

Joanna Constantinidis: stoneware pots with dry, textured glaze, three and a half inches high. After throwing, they were cut from their bases, flattened and welded onto flat slab bases

Hylton Nel and John Nowers: *left*, figures made of white earthenware clay, about four inches high, with moveable arms. The pattern is painted on transparent glaze with coloured glazes and underglaze colours.

Below, red earthenware bowl about six inches across. To make the inlay pattern, coloured clays were rolled into a slab of red clay pressed over a mould. On the outside of the bowl, a footring was added, a pattern incised, and the rim decorated. A transparent glaze on the inside completes this unusual pot

2 Weigh all the balls of clay you use and learn how much clay is needed to make a given size. Experienced potters rely on accurately weighed balls of clay for the evenness of repetition work. Knock clay into even balls and keep them wrapped in a sheet of plastic or a damp cloth to prevent them drying out.

3 2lb lumps of clay are a good starting point for beginners.

Tools (figure 16)
Personal tools are essential. To begin with I would suggest the following: a plain wire and a twisted wire; wooden tool with a pointed end; small soft sponge; needle firmly fixed in the end of a cork; bowl of clean water; 12in ruler and a strip of chamois leather. All tools should be kept clean.

The wheel
For the beginner, an electric wheel is by far the easiest to work. Manually operated wheels are difficult to use even for the skilled potter, let alone the beginner. Throwing is a fine skill, which needs a properly adjusted and efficient machine. Suppliers of wheels are listed in the back of the book.

Basic requirements are that the wheel must be firm and solid. If electric, it must give slow even speeds without loss of torque and be capable of throwing weights of clay of 10lb (or more). Kick wheels must be efficient in that the gear system must enable the kicking to be done regularly and evenly without causing the whole of the body to move. A reasonably heavy flywheel is essential and wheels that have a seat are usually the best. Wheel plans can be bought from which to build your own wheel. Kick wheels do allow greater control over the movement of the wheel though initially they are quite tiring to operate.

E

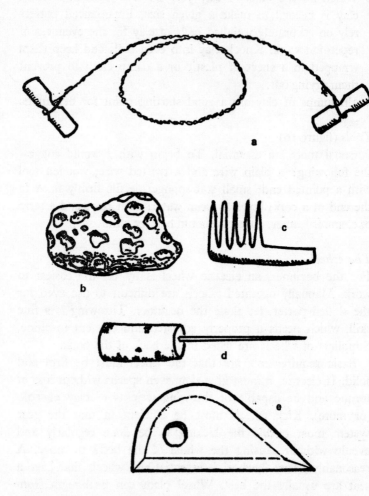

Figure 16 Tools a Twisted wire b Natural sponge c Comb
d Needle in cork e Wooden 'rib' tool

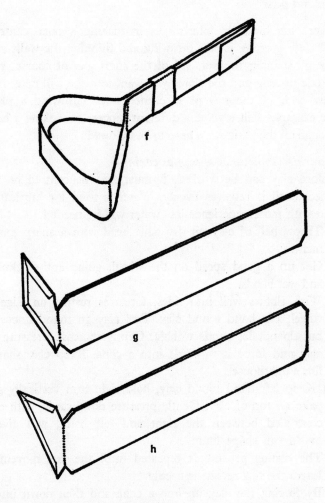

Figure 16 f Turning tool made from banding wire   g Square ended turning tool   h Triangular turning tool

Making pots

There are basically four stages in making a pot: centring the clay, opening it out, throwing and thinning the walls and, finally, shaping the pot. All of the steps are, of course, part of one process and the shape you want to make will determine how each of these steps is carried out. Throwing a plate, for example, will involve a different process to making a bowl though all the basic steps have to be followed.

Centring (sometimes known as coning)
Before clay can be worked, it must first be centred on the wheel until it revolves evenly. Water is used for lubrication and with more experience less water will be needed.

1 Throw ball of clay on dry wheelhead with a sharp movement.
2 Get up a good speed on the wheel, going anti-clockwise, and wet hands.
3 With elbows well into sides, forearms resting on edge of wheel, put hand round clay. Feel clay go round unevenly but do not let hands wobble. Gently increase pressure on clay and force it upwards into a cone. Keep clay shaped like a lighthouse.
4 Keep left hand round clay, hold right arm vertically and palm on top of clay. Gentle pressure downwards, with clay controlled between the right and left hand, will give a mushroom shape lump.
5 The coning process is repeated until the last movement leaves the clay revolving evenly.

By forcing the clay up into a cone and then down into a mushroom it is centred evenly throughout the lump. This procedure must be carried out successfully before moving into the next stage, though for large lumps of clay it is modified slightly.

Opening out

Depending on how large the lump of clay is, and the shape which is to be made, the opening out procedure is modified accordingly. The following method is for tall shapes or bowls from medium sized lumps of clay below 5 or 7lb.

1 Medium wheel speed, and with left hand round the clay, hold right arm vertically and rest fingers on left hand.
2 Gently push right hand thumb down centre of clay and push outwards to form the base of pot. Try to do this in a single movement. This movement forms the base and is made with the shape of the finished pot in mind.
3 Wrap right hand round pot, hold left arm vertical, put left hand thumb on right hand, and fingers on inside. With the left forefinger gently lift upwards the roll of clay which should be formed on the inside wall.
4 Always take hands and fingers off clay gently. Sudden movements can easily knock it off centre. Only touch clay when it is moving.

For opening larger lumps of clay or as an alternative centring method:

1 Medium wheel speed.
2 Wrap both hands round centred clay, curl thumbs on top of clay and gently push them down centre of lump.
3 Gently open the lump by pulling outwards with thumbs. A good thick wall should be made which can be lifted slightly with the fingers of the left hand.

Opening out is a vital part of throwing and must be mastered before moving on to the next stage. Uneven opening will result in a wobbly pot with the wall coming up unevenly and probably off centre. It is almost impossible to rectify uneven opening out.

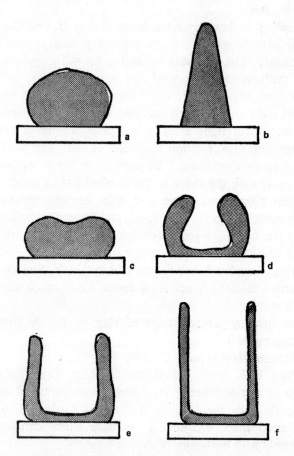

Figure 17 Throwing a cylinder   a Clay thrown on to wheel-head
b Squeezed up into cone   c Pressed down into mushroom   d Opened-
out   e Opened-out further and beginning of throwing   f Clay thrown-up
to form walls

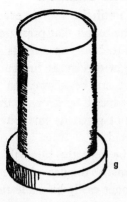

g Finished cylinder on wheel-head

Throwing and thinning

When the clay has been successfully opened out, then, depending on the shape required, throwing and thinning are carried out (see figure 17). Essentially, the throwing must be carried out with the finished shape firmly in mind. Plain cylinders are excellent shapes on which to practice, but their straight sides are not quite as easy to make as they look. Once a shape has spread out it is difficult to bring it back, therefore the throwing must be essentially a growing movement with each part of the pot moving towards the final shape. The following method is for straight sided cylinders.

1 Medium-slow wheel speed.

2 Keep arms and hands firm. Tuck elbows into sides and rest forearms on edge of wheel whenever possible.

3 Right hand should be on outside of pot, forefingers curled round and pushed into bottom of pot. Left hand is inside, forefinger curled round opposite right forefinger. A slight bulge of clay should be made above the fingers. This roll of clay is gradually brought to top of pot and pressure is gently released.

4 Repeat process until the wall is evenly thick from top to bottom. It will be found that pressure from the inside forefinger will help to bring up surplus clay from the bottom and reduce weight of clay at the bottom of the pot.

5 A cylinder must not be allowed to spread out; this tendency can be reduced by keeping the top slightly narrow and the pot is not given its final shape until the throwing has been completed.

6 The rim must be kept the same thickness as rest of pot. Rims can be made thinner at the end of throwing if required but cannot easily be made thicker. It can be made round and even by holding fingers on the two edges and smoothed with a wet strip of chamois.

COLLARING If the cylinder does spread slightly it can be brought in by the collaring process.

1 Medium wheel speed. Occasionally a fast wheel speed will be found best, depending on the state of the clay and thickness of the walls.

2 Wrap thumbs and forefingers round pot at bottom and moving slowly up the pot squeeze in the walls. This has to be done gently and a little at a time.

3 Repeat until walls are brought inwards.

TRIMMING If the top of the pot has come up unevenly it can be trimmed level with a needle or a taut wire.

1 Medium-slow wheel speed.

2 Support clay on inside with left hand, cut into outside with needle.

3 Lift sharply to remove surplus clay.

Shaping and finishing

A pot cannot arbitrarily be given any shape on the wheel.

The whole throwing process must be worked out from the start with a particular shape in mind. The following notes will act as a guide.

1 To make a shape go outward sufficient clay must be left so that the wall is not stretched beyond its capabilities as it will split. The movement out is both a throwing and a pushing one. Throwing must take place with the pressure from the inside being greater than that on the outside.

2 The shape can be made to go inwards by collaring as described earlier but this should be combined with throwing inwards as both techniques are used together. An increase in the wheel speed will often be found to be helpful with this movement.

3 A useful exercise based on a cylindrical form is to first design and then make a whole series of shapes using the same amount of clay (about 3lb). The first group of shapes could be based on cylinders with straight sides, the second group on full bodied shapes, the third group on shapes with fullness at the top and the last group with fullness at the bottom.

4 When making teapot spouts or small pots which are to be enclosed completely at the top, such as salt pots, the following notes should help.

   a The clay must be extra soft; the softer the easier it is to throw.

   b Wheel at fast speed throughout the process.

   c As far as possible keep the shape a miniature of the required shape from the start, and make it grow to the necessary size.

   d For spouts, a wooden tool can be used on the inside if the pot is too small or your finger cannot reach down.

   e To close the top of a small pot leave a good roll of clay at the rim, support the top from the inside with your left forefinger and throw the wall over your finger inwards, and slightly upwards.

f Squeeze the top together with the finger ends and with slight downward pressure close the hole.

g The shape can be changed slightly by using a wooden tool on the outside. Air trapped inside will prevent the walls collapsing.

5 Narrow necks on large pots can be made in two ways. The method explained above of collaring-in and throwing the walls can be used, or the neck can be thrown on the pot after it has hardened slightly. In this technique the bottom part of the pot is allowed to harden slightly, a coil of soft clay is then added and thrown into the required shape. Alternatively, the bottom and neck of the pot can be thrown quite separately and luted together when they have stiffened slightly.

A wooden tool held against the side of the pot will remove slurry and can also be used to make final adjustments to the shape. The bottom of the pot, when it joins the wheelhead, needs to be trimmed down with a wooden tool to remove surplus clay preparatory to the pot being removed from the wheel.

The surface of the pot can be finished in one of several ways. Throwing rings which occur while the pot is being made can either be left or be smoothed over with your fingers or a potter's rib. Whether the marks are left or not is a matter of preference but as a guide, the throwing rings should be used to enhance the form and as such, have to be carefully considered within the total effect of the finished pot.

Removing pots from the wheel

Small pots can be moved from the wheelhead quickly and

with little fuss. They may however be difficult to remove if they have taken a long time to make and the clay has become too soft. Large pots, large bowls and plates cannot be lifted off the wheelhead and should be made on a batt which is temporarily fixed to the wheelhead and removed when the pot is made.

Small pots

1 Flood the stationary wheelhead with clean water and cut underneath the pot with a plain wire. Repeat if necessary.
2 Using fingers of both hands gently push the base of pot across the wheelhead so that pot slides off the wheel and on to a piece of asbestos or tile.

USING A SCRAPER

1 Cut under pot with a twisted wire.
2 Wet a clean paint scraper with clean water, ease up base of pot and slide scraper underneath.
3 Put pot on asbestos batt or tile.

LIFTING

1 Pots which are to be lifted off the wheel must be made fairly quickly so that the clay is not too soft, and any slurry must be removed from the sides with wooden tool.
2 Cut under pot with twisted wire.
3 Clean and dry your hands and gently grip pot near base with both hands. Lift pot up, tilting it slightly to avoid suction.
4 With small bowls, the finger ends will usually be sufficient.

Large Pots

Some wheelheads have fittings which hold specially made batts in position; when this is the case, throwing proceeds

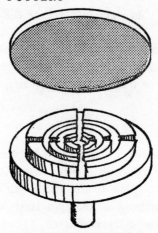

Figure 18 Fixing batt on to a prepared chuck of clay

as usual and a twisted wire is pulled under the completed pot to allow it to contract without splitting.

To fit batts on an ordinary wheelhead a chuck has to be made (figure 18).

1 Use medium soft clay, centre and spread clay out flat on the wheelhead using the edge of your right hand supported by your left hand. The chuck needs to be about ⅝in thick.

2 Cut concentric circles in the flat clay with a wooden tool. Stop wheel and cut a cross in the chuck.

3 Batts can be made out of varnished marine plywood or asbestos. Wet the batt slightly before placing it in position. A firm tap in the centre should be sufficient to hold it in place. Test to see the batt is flat and tap it as necessary. Some potters recommend the use of plaster of Paris batts soaked in water but such batts lack mechanical strength and, if knocked, chips of plaster may get into the clay.

4 When the pot is made, cut under it with a twisted wire. The batt can then be removed and the chuck re-used.

Plates (figure 19)

Small plates and saucers can be removed from the wheelhead by either lifting with a scraper or, if the clay is very plastic, with your hands. Large plates of over 9in diameter usually need to be thrown on a batt. The normal centring movements are carried out but the final movement is done by the edge of the right hand pressing the clay downwards and outwards to form the first stage in making the plate. Too much pressure at this stage will make the centre of the base of the plate too thin, too little and it will be too thick. Sufficient clay must be left in a roll at the edge of the plate to make a rim.

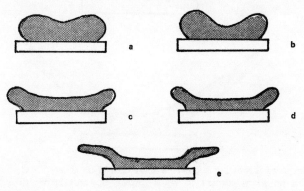

Figure 19 Throwing a plate a Clay central on wheel b Opening out movement c Clay flattened leaving bulge at edge d Edges left to form rim e Rim formed as final movement

Bowls (figure 20)

Unlike making cylinders, the opening out movement, when making a bowl, is not intended to make a base but rather to show where the walls start. Most good bowls have no base, as such, and the internal profile is smooth and even.

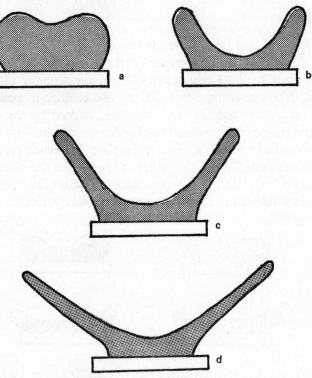

Figure 20 Throwing a bowl a Clay central on wheel b Opening-out with no sharp corners c Walls thrown upwards rather than outwards d Final movements spread out the bowl

1 Medium soft clay, centring method as usual.
2 Open the clay out with your right thumb pushed down the centre or use your two thumbs, but do not making a swing-ing-out movement.
3 For small bowls the sides need to be pulled upwards and outwards and the shape is completed finally when the throwing has been done. Straight sided walls can be thrown much more easily than those which are curved.

4 If the bowl is to be tall and deep, keep the shape more cylindrical, but ensure that sufficient clay is left especially at the rim, to allow the bowl to be thrown in its full form.

5 For bowls which are flat and wide, the base needs to be made wider to support the walls and prevent them collapsing during throwing. The final pull outwards to give the bowl its maximum width should not be made until all the other throwing is complete.

Lids and lips

Lids can be fitted in a variety of ways and it is only a question of choosing the lid most suitable for the pot. Functional as well as aesthetic reasons have to be borne in mind. For example a teapot lid must fit firmly when the teapot is in use as well as suiting the style of pot.

Housings for lids (figure 21)
Housings or seatings for lids are partially made soon after the clay has been opened up and the walls have begun to be made. A roll of clay should be left for the seating and a depression made in it with the end of the left forefinger. As the walls are thrown higher the seating is left undisturbed until the throwing is completed. Finally the seating is sharpened and defined using the finger end or a wooden tool.

Lids
Well fitting lids depend on accurate measurements of both the lid and the seating as well as using clay in the same state as that used for the body of the pot. Measurements can be taken with a ruler or calipers.

Small lids for such things as teapots can be thrown in

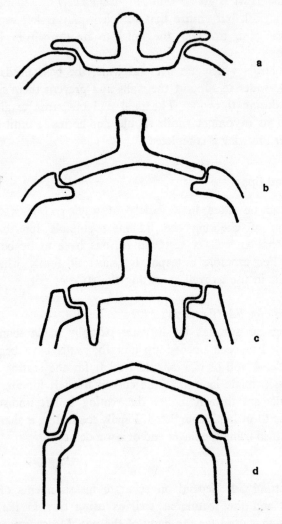

Figure 21 Types and fitting of lids   a Sunk lid   b Flat inset lid
c Flange lid   d Cover

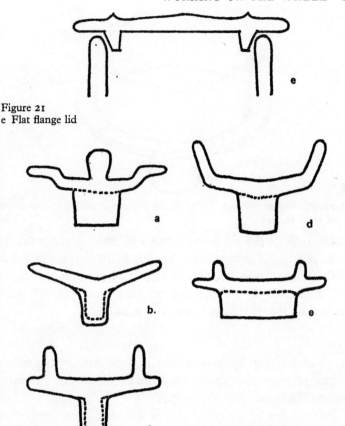

Figure 21
e Flat flange lid

Figure 22 How lids shown in figure 21 are made on wheel

different ways depending on their shape, some are thrown upside down and some the right way up (see figure 22). The diagram will help to make this point clearer. For example, lid *a* is thrown the right way up while the lids *b, c, d* and *e* are thrown upside down. Teapot lids must remain securely in position when tea is poured from the pot. If the flange on the

F

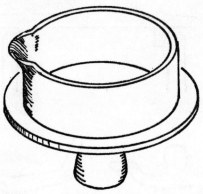

Figure 23 Teapot lid with pulled lip to prevent it falling out of teapot when tea is poured

underneath of the lid is large this will often prevent the lid from falling out, otherwise a lip can be made on the flange while it is still soft which will keep it in position (see figure 23). Casserole lids, depending on their size, can either be lifted from the wheelhead or made on a batt.

Lips

A good pouring lip is one which does not dribble either during or after use. There are no rules which can guarantee success but these notes may help.

1 Pull out the lip while the clay is still soft. It can be further enlarged if necesary when the clay has stiffened.

2 Make the lip larger than you actually want as lips have a tendency to spring back into their original position while drying. Pull in the sides of the lip so that a funnel is formed to channel the liquid.

Turning

Most thrown pots need turning on the wheel to remove

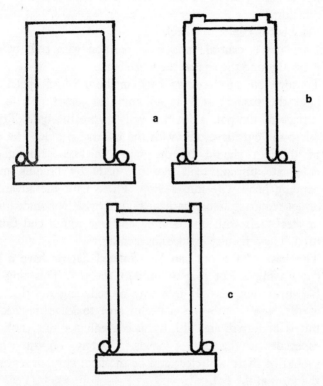

Figure 24 Turning a cylinder   a Base turned flat   b Foot rim set under base   c Foot rim set on edge of base

surplus clay, tidy up the base and give the pot its final shape. The turning process is carried out on the leather-hard pots which are replaced upside down on the wheel and clay is trimmed off with a metal tool.

Straightforward pots (figure 24)

1 Pots should be leather-hard. If the clay is too soft it will

not cut away easily or cleanly. If it is too hard, turning is difficult.

2 Place pot in centre of wheel.

3 Once pot is central, hold it in position with coils of clay pressed round the rim on the wheelhead.

4 To turn off surplus clay have medium wheel speed and hold the turning tool at an angle of about 60° to the surface of the pot. Trim the walls before the base. Try to relate the outside profile with the internal profile. The wall of the pot should be the same thickness throughout. Adequate turning tools can be made by binding metal banding hoop wire into a loop. These have the advantage of not requiring to be sharpened. Otherwise loop-ended tools or steel tools with one pointed and one round end can be used. These require regular sharpening.

5 The base of the pot can be trimmed flat or have a foot cut leaving a foot ring to support the pot. This ring fulfils three functions. It is a way of reducing the thickness of the base, it provides a useful area to leave unglazed if this is preferred, and, thirdly, it can enhance the whole pot especially in the case of bowls. Turning, on the whole, should be sharp and clear and be the final stage in revealing the form of the pot.

6 When grogged clay has been turned, it may be necessary to smooth over the surface with a wooden tool or the edge of a knife held close to the surface.

Small fine bowls

Fine bowls are easily damaged by coils of clay pressed round the side. The alternative method to that of holding them in position on the wheelhead with coils of clay is to flatten a ball of clay on the centre of the wheel and turn it perfectly flat. On this place the bowl, and tap it into central position. Gently tap middle of base to fix bowl onto pad of clay and turn as usual.

Repetition turning

This is the easiest and quickest method whenever there are a quantity of similar pots to turn. A clay support known as a chuck, on which the pots sit, is made on the wheelhead. A tall chuck (figure 25) is required for mugs and other tall shapes and a flat open chuck for plates.

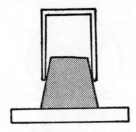

Figure 25 Chuck for supporting straight sided pots when turning

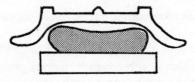

Figure 26 Chuck supporting turned plate showing foot rim and central bump of clay which prevents plate sagging in kiln.

The solid chuck is made using medium-hard wedged clay placed as centrally as possible on the wheelhead and finally turned even. The taper on the chuck must be as slight as possible otherwise the pot will tend to push into the chuck and form an uneven groove. The chuck for holding plates on the wheel (figure 26) is best made by placing on the wheel-

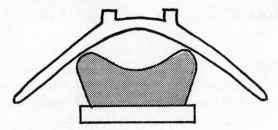

Figure 27 Chuck supporting turned bowl

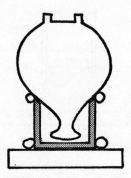

Figure 28 Method of supporting narrow necked pot for turning

head a thick coil of clay. This is turned to fit the inside profile of the plate which is subsequently tapped gently into position on the chuck. Large bowls can also be turned on a chuck (figure 27).

Narrow necked pots
Pots which cannot be inverted on their rims for some reason, such as narrow necked pots, can be turned by placing them inside a hollow chuck which supports the walls rather than the top of the pot (figure 28). The chuck can be made from either a suitable sized fired pot fixed in position on the

wheelhead with coils of clay, or it can be specially made from medium hard clay, turned even at the top to hold the pot.

Knobs on lids

Thrown lids can be left with sufficient clay to enable knobs to be turned, or can have a knob thrown onto the turned lid by the following method.

1 Turn lid and leave in position on wheel.
2 Prepare clay for knob as soft as can be handled satisfactorily and make into a small ball.
3 Scratch centre of lid, push on knob and lute sides into lid.
4 Maximum wheel speed, moisten fingers and gently centre clay using a wooden tool if necessary. Avoid wetting remainder of lid and work as quickly as possible.
5 Pierce a hole into knob through inside of lid to prevent knob being blown off in kiln by trapped air.

Because the clay used in thrown knobs is softer than the rest of the lid, it will shrink more than the lid and needs to be larger to compensate for this. Unfired clay lids are easier to pick up than glazed and fired ones and this also needs to be taken into account when size is being considered. Holes in teapot lids are to let in air as tea comes out through the spout and can be cut with an inverted pen nib in a pen holder or similar tool.

Assembling pots

Teapots and casseroles are assembled shapes in that handles and lids are fitted to the basic pot (figure 29). Such arrangements call for considerable technical as well as aesthetic skill. Technical, in that all joins must be firm, neat and clean. Aesthetic, in that each unit must be part of the whole and

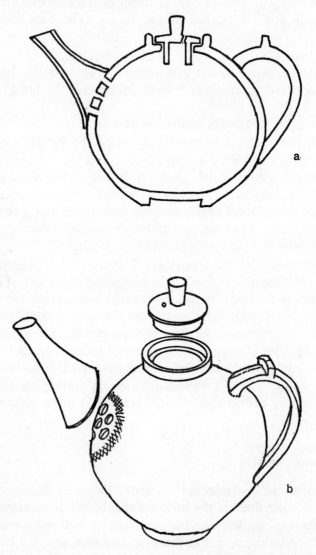

Figure **29** Teapot a Cross-section of teapot b Assembling a teapot

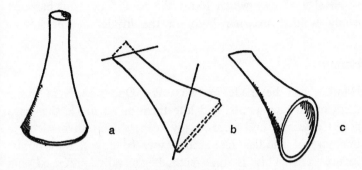

Figure 30 Making a spout   a Thrown spout   b Cut spout   c Spout
ready for fixing on to pot

fit in as such. A knife with a curved blade may be found helpful to trim teapot spouts (figure 30) which should be in the
same state of hardness as the pot. Keeping the spout inside
the teapot will help the spout to retain moisture until fired
into position.

Oval dishes

Oval dishes can be made in two ways depending on their size.
Small oval dishes, say up to 10in diameter, are thrown in the
usual way, lifted off the wheel and put down on a thin
sprinkling of sand. As soon as the pot can be handled without
damage, but before it is leather-hard, a leaf-shaped piece is
cut out of the bottom of the pot and the two cut surfaces
are scratched and painted with slurry. The outside of the
base is pressed inwards to close up the hole and the join luted
firmly together, inside and out.

Large oval dishes are made from wheel thrown pots which
have the base cut off; then, when the walls have stiffened
slightly they are pushed in an oval shape and stood on a pre-

pared slab of clay which forms the base. Sides and base are firmly welded together both on the inside and outside.

Handles

Handles can be made in two ways. One way is to throw them much like spouts, and lute them on to the leather-hard pot. Casseroles and occasionally teapots lend themselves to this sort of handle. The second way is to pull the handles (figure 31). This is the method generally preferred and handles on mugs and so on are made in this way by the following method.

1 Prepare clay harder than usual and cut it into long blocks about 1½in wide and 8in long.
2 Hold block vertically in left hand and stroke it with the wet right hand into a long strap-like shaped handle.
3 With the end of the right thumb, nip handle from the block and lay handle on a wooden board to stiffen slightly before fixing it to the pot.
4 To fix the handle into position, scratch pot, tap end of handle to thicken it, moisten end and push it firmly in position and weld it neatly on to the pot.
5 Hold pot horizontal with the left hand and stroke handle straight with the right hand.
6 Stand pot on edge of table and gently bend handle round and fix base firmly on to pot with a swift clean movement.

Pulled handles can be bent over on to themselves and allowed to stiffen slightly before being fixed onto the pot (figure 32).

Handles can also be cut with a wire template pulled through a block a clay and fixed to pot in the way described above (figure 33).

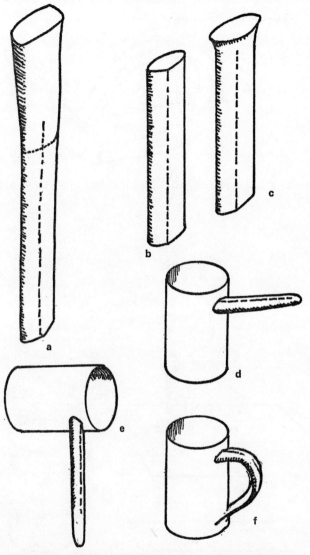

Figure 31 Making and fixing a pulled handle a Clay stroked to form handle b Handle nipped off at dotted line c End of handle thickened by tapping d Handle pushed on to mug e Mug held horizontally while handle is stroked to final shape

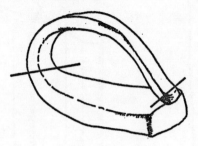

Figure 32 Pulled handle allowed to harden slightly before being applied to pot

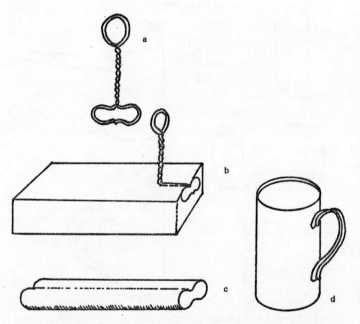

Figure 33 Making a wire-pulled handle   a Shape made from strong wire   b Pulling wire through prepared clay   c Handle   d Handle fixed on to pot

Decorative thrown ware

As well as functional pots, the wheel can be used for making shapes which can be altered in many ways. For some potters, the pots made on the wheel are ends in themselves, but for other potters these are only the beginning. I suggest here a few of the possible ways in which pots thrown on the wheel can be treated.

Bashing Pots can be bashed and tapped with different effects in almost any state other than when dry. Soft pots can be pushed, while stiffer ones need tapping or beating with a wooden stick. To make shapes other than round, cut off the base which prevents free movement of the walls, and when form is completed weld it to a slab base.

Carving A favourite Japanese and Chinese method of changing the shape of pots was to carve them with a thin sharp knife or clay plane of some sort. A 'Surform' tool is suitable for this. The necessary thickness must be allowed for in the walls and carving or shaving is best done when the walls are leather-hard.

Joining Thrown pots can be cut into many different shapes and can be re-arranged to form a wide variety of sculptural forms. A pot can be used as the basis of the form with parts of other pots added to it, or the cut shapes can be joined together and built up into the form. For example, pots can be sliced down the middle and joined back to back. The quality which the technique of throwing gives to clay can be exploited by this method of cutting up the pots.

6

Decoration

Useful pottery has to fulfil certain definite functions. Once these requirements have been completed further treatment of the pot becomes, on a purely practical basis, unnecessary. However, potters have rarely been concerned only with the functional aspect of pottery. Almost since pots have been made, they have been decorated in some way or another.

The Chinese potters of the Sung period kept decoration work down to a minimum using simple lines and applied relief on strong forms with plain glazes. Later, Chinese potters found delight in painting on their pots in blue pigment to produce the famous blue and white wares of the Ming period. The urge to decorate was also very pronounced in Islamic pottery which was often decorated with swirling geometrical patterns in rich colours. This pottery in turn influenced the Spanish and Italian potters. Much of the pottery made commercially during the nineteenth century in England was highly coloured and heavily decorated.

It is however, to the work of the small country potteries that we look for some of the great examples of English pottery. These country potters made pots for a local market, used locally obtained materials, usually very limited in range and produced functional wares for a discriminating though comparatively poor population. Apart from the functional ware, they made large pots or dishes which were richly decorated for special occasions such as weddings or christenings. Most of this work is greatly admired today. It was made from simple forms with a limited range of materials. Decoration usually consisted of different coloured clays under a transparent glaze. Such work, usually known as slip-ware, reached the peak of its achievement in Staffordshire at the end of the seventeenth century. In these pots, the joy and skill of the potter, who found pleasure in decorating his work without detracting from its basic simplicity, can be seen.

Here too, all the ' principles ' of decoration are evident. The form for example was always strong and dominant. A weak form will not be made strong by clever decoration, though a strong form can be weakened by unsuitable or inappropriate decoration. The decoration on the pots was straightforward in that a limited technique was exploited to its fullest extent. No attempts were made to combine different decorative techniques on the same pot. Though it is possible to generalize about decoration, there are, in fact, no hard and fast rules; the only criterion that can safely be used is whether or not the total effect of the decoration works. While this is always a personal decision, much can be learned from studying the classical pots from China, or the English slip-wares of the seventeenth century.

In this chapter all the different decorating techniques which can be used on the pot before it is fired are explored. The use of glaze and coloured pigments is explained in Chapter 7. For the sake of clarity each technique is described separately and though it is often best to select and concentrate on only one technique, all can be used in combination.

Clay with clay

Simple modelled decoration can be carried out while the clay is plastic and this is, perhaps, the most immediate sort of decoration. For example, the clay can be pinched into ridges and grooves; tools, fingers or thumb nails can be pressed into the clay or the edge of the pot can be undulated. Most of these decorative techniques can be practised on flat tiles to give regular patterned or textured effects.

Following this direct method of applied decoration the whole pot can be treated as one decorative unit. For example, ribs can be pinched in the walls of the pot, like those used in nature to give strength (figure 34). Poppy heads, for example,

Figure 34 Two thumb pots joined together and decorated with applied clay

are an excellent source of inspiration for decorative as well as functional form. There are many other examples from nature which are an inspiration for this sort of decoration: gourds, acorns, maize, hazelnuts and pomegranates.

The method of treating the whole pot decoratively is used by the potter Sheila Fournier, who makes bowls in this sort of way. She adds strips of clay to the rim or walls of the bowls and these often contract more than the pot. The cracks and splits which occur are incorporated as a feature of the bowl.

Incised

Decoration which is cut into or pressed into the surface is known as incised decoration. It can be carried out while the clay is leather-hard or plastic. Scratched decoration made with a comb or similar tool is a type of incised decoration which can be carried out freely or can be banded into the pot while it revolves on the potter's wheel or on a banding wheel.

Fine detailed decoration cut or scratched into the clay rarely benefits from being glazed as this covers up much of the detail. It is often better left totally unglazed or painted with a pigment with a matt surface such as manganese or iron oxides.

Carving

Clay can only be carved successfully when leather-hard. A variety of tools can be used such as knives, planes, Surform tool and chisels and, providing the clay is of sufficient thickness, the carving can be reasonably deep. Formal patterns of repeating designs can be carved as well as more naturalistically rendered scenes.

Inlaying

Inlaying is a method of decoration in which leather-hard clay is impressed or incised with patterns, which are filled with clay of a contrasting colour to the body until the impression is completely filled. When the inlay is leather-hard it can be scraped level with the surface of the pot. Medieval potters used this technique on tiles which were used for pavements especially in churches and abbeys. In Korea the inlay tech-

G

nique of ' Mishima ' was developed, in which finely incised patterns were inlaid with either dark brown or white clay. The Korean work was fine and delicate in contrast to the bold stylized heraldic designs favoured by many of the medieval English potters. Nineteenth-century potters in Sussex pressed printers' type into the red clay and inlaid the designs with white clay. Almost any tool can be used to make the pattern provided the edges are kept sharp and crisp and neat.

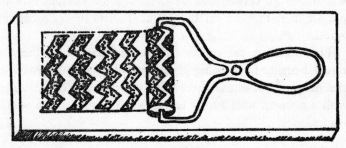

Figure 35 Carved plaster of Paris or wooden roller tool for decorating clay

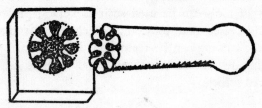

Figure 36 Decorative clay stamp

Rollers and stamps (figures 35 and 36)
Small round rollers of wood carved with a simple geometrical design can be rolled over clay before it is leather-hard to give either a patterned or textured surface. In parts of Nigeria small rollers woven out of cord or straw are used to this day to make such patterns.

Stamps can be made out of clay or wood for special designs. It is a tradition for all pots to be stamped with the mark of the potter. This stamp, or seal as it is known, can take the form of a decorative device, or the initials or name. Stamps for impressing small designs can be made out of metal, wood or clay. The Chinese at one time made stamps out of metal which were pressed very slightly into the clay. The design was fully revealed when covered with a tinted transparent glaze which, in the kiln, thickened and darkened in the design, and subtly picked it out.

Other stamps can be made from such things as shells, pine cones or string stuck on to a wooden block. Almost any simple textured objects can be successfully used.

Burnishing

Sometimes called polishing, burnishing is a method of giving pots a smooth, flat, shiny surface without using a glaze. The leather-hard surface of the pot is rubbed in a circular movement with a smooth object such as a pebble. Red clay, which contains iron oxide, can be burnished most effectively. No glaze is applied to the pot or the effect of the burnishing is lost.

Applied

Clay can be applied to pots in a number of decorative ways.

1 Thin coils of soft clay can be stuck with slurry on the pot before it becomes leather-hard. These coils can be pressed to form a pattern or be incised with wooden tools. Small balls of clay can be applied in the same way.

2 Clay of a different colour can be applied as decoration. Care will have to be taken to ensure that the two clays will 'fit' together. This means both clays must shrink at the same rate and by the same amount. You may be lucky

and find two different clays which will hold together or it may possible to stain clay used for the body of the pot. Using slurry which is a mixture of both clays will also help to strengthen the join.

3 Clay pushed through a coarse sieve gives a pleasant curled effect of fine strands and can be used decoratively on pots.

Modelling

Pots have often been modelled with anthropomorphic features. Such modelling must be done before the pot has become leather-hard to prevent it cracking off and, to be successful from the point of view of design it should be related to the form of the pot in some way. Such modelling can be humorous, satirical, serious and so on.

Colouring oxides

Clays and glazes are stained and coloured by metal oxides. These are bought prepared as fine powders, usually coloured brown or black in their raw state. The colour of the unfired oxide is usually no indication of its fired colour. A list of colouring oxides is on pages 116-7; they can be painted directly on the pot in its unfired state but, at earthenware temperature, need to be subsequently covered with glaze. To make them less powdery mix them with a little dry powdered clay. Apply the pigment on to the dry pot in bold large brush strokes and try to make each brush stroke definite. It is a technique quite unlike that of painting on paper, as the clay, being very absorbent, dries the brush very quickly, and the result can look messy if done slowly or painted with the ' filling-in ' technique used in a colouring book.

Clay slip

One of the traditional English country wares is that known as slip-ware. The pots were usually made out of red clay, decorated with liquid clay slips of different colours, given a transparent glaze and fired to earthenware temperature. The slip is either poured or trailed on the pot in different ways and the directness of the method calls for a bold, quick approach which gives much of the work a fresh quality rarely found in other methods of decoration.

Preparing the slip

Slip can best be made from the same clay as that used for the pot, but this is not always possible. For example white slip usually has to be mixed quite separately from a special recipe. For all dark slips, however, use the body clay as the basis and add oxides to it.

1 Weigh out dry clay (unfired pots or clay which has dried out are suitable) together with required oxides. Full recipes are given on page 102.
2 Add clay (in small pieces) and oxides to bucket of water and leave to soak for a day.
3 Stir mixture regularly until all clay is softened. Put through 80 mesh sieve, brushing it through with stiff brush. Sieve the mixture three times or until all the lumps have been broken up. At this stage keep the slip very thin as this makes it much easier to prepare.
4 Leave slip to settle and syphon off unwanted water. For pouring, the slip should have the consistency of cream, but it needs to be thicker for trailing.
5 Stir slip well before use and store in a lidded bucket; after use, scrape sides of bucket with a rubber kidney to prevent slip drying and falling as lumps into the bucket.

Slips must expand and contract by the same amount as the clay and at the same rate, otherwise they crack or flake off. This problem arises more often with white slips as they sometimes need to be mixed from three or four ingredients. Several recipes may have to be tried out until a satisfactory slip is found. Label buckets clearly stating the colour of the slip and, if necessary, its recipe. Slip and glazes often look alike in their raw state and need to be clearly marked. Some pottery suppliers make slip stains which are used to colour the slip instead of oxides and give a wider variety of colours. The manufacturers usually give complete instructions as to the amount required for various shades.

Slip recipes
Figures express proportions by weight

1	**Brown Slip**		5	**Blue Slip**	
	Red clay	100		White ball clay	80
2	**Tan Slip**			Feldspar	15
	Red clay	55		Red clay	5
	Ball clay	45		Cobalt oxide	3
3	**White Slip**			Copper oxide	½
a	White ball clay	80		Manganese oxide	½
	Feldspar	20	6	**Black Slip**	
b	White ball clay	80		Red clay	100
	China clay	20		Iron oxide	6
4	**Green Slip**			Copper oxide	3
	White ball clay	80		Manganese	3
	Feldspar	20			
	Copper oxide	5			
	Cobalt oxide	1			

Applying slips
Slips can only be applied to clay which is in a suitable condition. Most clays will withstand slip when they are leather-hard, providing they are not totally immersed. Slip has a softening effect on leather-hard pots and when large areas need to be covered, it has to be done quickly and carefully.

It is helpful to wax the foot to prevent slip from adhering when it is being poured over the pot. When it is planned to dip the whole of the outside of the pot, some potters make the shape of the pot accordingly and leave a foot ring to provide the finger with a good grip on the pot itself.

DIPPING Fairly large quantities of slip are required if pots are to be dipped, but dipping is the most satisfactory method of covering pots evenly. If the pot is to be covered with slip on both the inside and the outside, the inside is slipped first and allowed to become leather-hard before the outside is dipped. The inside is slipped by swilling round a small quantity and pouring out the surplus. To cover the outside, the pot is held level, to prevent slip going inside and gently dipped into the slip. Many clays have a tendency to bloat when both walls of a pot are dipped in slip at the same time.

POURING When only small quantities of slip are available or when limited areas are to be covered, the slip can be poured over the walls of the pot. This is best done by holding the pot firmly over a large bowl and pouring slip down the walls.

When bowls or other flat ware such as plates are to be slipped on the inside, it is much safer to do this before they have been turned, as the thicker walls makes handling them much easier.

FLAT SURFACES Slabs of clay are ideal for slip decoration. Slabs to be slipped should be laid on a cloth on a board which can be tipped to enable the clay to be swirled over the surface.

TRAILING Slip which is slightly thicker than that used

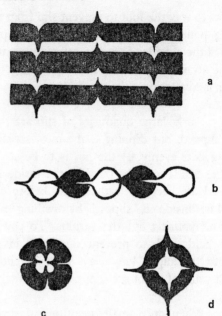

Figure 37 Slip-trailed decoration   a 'Feathering'   b 'Chain'
c 'Flower'   d 'Star'

for pouring can be trailed in much the same way as icing sugar is piped on a cake (figure 37). Any sort of trailer can be used provided it allows a regular and even flow of slip from a nozzle of some sort. Enema syringes are ideal. So are plastic bottles fitted with nozzles. Flat collapsible balloon type rubber bags fitted with nozzles are also suitable. Some potters use babies' feeding bottles. The Staffordshire potters made their own slip trailers out of clay.

Slip trailed directly on leather-hard clay gives clear definition with slip lines standing on top of the surface of the clay. This method can be used successfully on vertical surfaces though it requires dexterity and speed. Slip can be trailed on to a wet slip ground, in the technique known as wet on wet. In this process the slip lines lose a little definition and lie in, rather than on, the background, but the fluid soft quality of the technique comes out fully when this method is used. Slip can be either trailed in straight lines close to each other and 'feathered' which involve pulling a fine bristle across the trailed lines, or applied as dots which can also be 'feathered' from the centre outwards, or from the outside inwards. Complex patterns can be carried out quite easily on flat slabs which, when leather-hard, can be used in moulds and slab pots. Slip trailed on to wet vertical surfaces will run down very easily and this can be incorporated as a feature in the design.

Skill with the slip-trailer demands sure movements and designs which are relatively straightforward to carry out even if they are made up of complex patterns. Sweeping movements rather than small 'tight' movements will help to achieve the fresh quality of good slip decoration. Practice on bench tops, or biscuited or raw pots, is invaluable and will help to promote confidence.

MARBLING Different coloured slips can be swirled together to form a marbled pattern. The inside of bowls and dishes particularly lend themselves to this sort of slip decoration and, if carefully chosen and applied slips are used together, the effect can be very rich. Trailed designs, if they become messy can, as a last resort, be swirled to form a marbled pattern.

SGRAFFITO The technique of scratching designs through a layer of slip to show the body underneath is known as sgraffito. When the slip is dry, hard, uneven lines result; when it is leather-hard, the lines are cleaner and have greater sharpness. Larger areas of slip can be removed with small metal chisel-like tools in the technique known as 'champlevé'. Designs can be drawn on the slip in pencil as these burn away in the firing.

WAX RESIST Hot wax can be used to resist areas of slip. Apart from its use on the foot of the pot, and on stoneware to prevent slip going on all surfaces which come into contact with each other, hot wax can be used decoratively to resist further coats of slip or colouring pigment. Paraffin wax mixed with a small quantity of paraffin gives a suitable mixture when heated. This can be done either over a candle or in a water bath, which is safer but limits the temperature of the wax. Some potters prefer a hot mixture of light machine oil and wax. A prepared wax emulsion can also be purchased which does not need heating but is painted on the pot and becomes water resistant when it is dry. It has the added convenience that brushes washed out in water immediately after use are not ruined.

LEAF RESIST A leaf pressed into clay can be painted over with a dark slip. When the leaf is removed a perfect silhouette is left which bears the impression of the veins of the leaf. If the pot has been made out of light coloured clay, a subsequent, tinted transparent glaze will thicken and darken slightly in the vein marks giving a very life-like effect. This technique was particularly popular with late nineteenth-century art potters in England and is now used by some Japanese potters.

PAPER RESIST The advantages of using paper to resist slip, instead of wax, is that the design can be carefully and meticulously worked out and paper can be used for hard-edged and soft-edged designs. Paper resist is usually used when the pot is leather-hard and on the inside of bowls before they have been turned.

1 Cut or tear paper to required shape and soak in water until quite saturated. Newspaper or duplicating paper is suitable.

2 Apply wet paper to pot and press gently into position. Keep paper moist by dabbing it with a wet sponge if necessary.

3 Slip pot as usual, either by pouring, painting or spraying. Leave paper in position and do not remove it until slip has lost its shine.

4 Edges of slip can either be left sharp or smoothed over with thumb, sponge or brush. Designs can be built up using several layers of different coloured slips. For geometrical designs, only one layer may be necessary.

Paper resist can also be used when the clay is softer than leather-hard. Stiff paper or thin card is pressed well into the surface of the clay so that definite impressions are made and these are heightened by the succeeding layer of slip.

7

Glazes and Glazing

Pottery is usually finished by being glazed. In this process, the pots are covered with a specially prepared glass mixture and fired for a second time in the kiln. During the firing, the glaze melts and forms a smooth, even, waterproof covering which makes the pot suitable for domestic use. There are many different types of glazes; some are shiny like glass while others are matt with a slightly textured surface. Glazes can be made in many different colours and can be applied in a wide variety of decorative techniques.

Quite simply, a glaze is a sort of glass made from materials which melt at high temperature. The most important ingredients of a glaze are those of silica and alumina which are forced to melt at the required temperature by the addition of another ingredient known as a flux, the choice of which is determined by the temperature at which the glaze is required to melt. Lead and borax are two fluxes which are used for earthenware. Calcium, magnesium and potassium are stoneware fluxes. Because lead is poisonous in its raw state and borax is soluble in water, both of these materials are prepared in the form of frits. These are industrially prepared in powdered form and are made by heating lead or borax with other materials until they melt to form a glass. This mixture is ground and used as an ordinary, but safe, glaze ingredient.

The use of different materials for different temperatures should make it apparent that earthenware and stoneware glazes are compounded from different materials and many raw materials are restricted in use to one particular field.

Buying prepared glazes

This is undoubtedly the simplest way for the beginner to start. Glaze manufacturers work to carefully calculated glaze recipes which are usually specially suited to clays they also supply. These glazes can form the basis of a whole series of experiments using only a limited range of materials. I suggest here a range of ideas which can be followed.

Earthenware
Basically there are two types of earthenware glaze, those with a lead flux, often known as low solubility glazes, and leadless glazes which are fluxed by borax and are known as alkaline glazes. Lead glazes are more reliable over a wider temperature range and cause oxides to give slightly different colours to those formed by the same oxides in an alkaline glaze. Some fired lead glazes are also slightly soluble in acid solutions (such as vinegar, orange or lemon juice) and must be fired to the recommended temperatures as well as being used according to any other stated instructions. Alkaline glazes, on the other hand, are perfectly safe to use being completely non-poisonous both before they are melted and afterwards, unlike lead which is poisonous unless fritted and must in any case be handled with care.

One basic glaze only need be purchased to begin with – a clear shiny transparent glaze firing to 1080°C or 1100°C. With this one glaze a variety of different effects can be obtained. When applied over red clay it appears dark brown:

over coloured slips it brings out their final colour depending on the oxides in the slip. It is an ideal glaze for slip-ware and from a practical point of view the smooth surface it gives is well suited to most domestic and functional ware. Small amounts of colouring oxides added to the clear glaze give coloured transparent glazes and these can be effectively used over light coloured bodies or white slip. The exact colour of the oxides will depend on the type of glaze, whether it contains lead or not. The chart on pages 116-7 lists in full the details and effects of the various oxides.

Tin oxide added to the basic glaze renders it white and opaque and gives the glaze commonly known as majolica. This was the glaze which was used extensively by the old Delft potters of Holland. White opaque glazes can be used over any clay and are ideal for painted decoration of all kinds. They can also be coloured with the addition of colouring oxides. Glazes rendered white with tin oxide become less fluid in the firing and must be applied to the pot more evenly for successful results. Opaque white glazes can be bought ready prepared from the suppliers.

Pottery suppliers list many other earthenware glazes. These tend to be less shiny and sometimes have matt or broken surfaces. They may be creamy-white or black-brown in colour. Experiments with such glazes and practice in deciding where to use them will provide the most valuable experience.

The so called 'art' glazes are usually listed separately in the suppliers' catalogues. They are not meant for general use on functional ware but for use on sculptural and decorative objects. Unfortunately, the effects of many of the glazes have a commercial 'spectacular' quality quite unrelated to the work of the home potter and are best left until a specific use is found for them.

Stoneware

Again, a commercially produced transparent glaze can form the basis of many exciting glazes. Lead is not used in stoneware glazes, and the glazes are far safer to handle. Basic ingredients of the glaze will affect any colouring oxides or other materials which are added, and what may be successful in one glaze may not be successful in another. Once experiments with stoneware glazes have been made most potters want to continue by making their own glazes based on some understanding of how the raw materials will react together; however, the prepared clear glazes can still play a useful part even for the experienced potter. Shoji Hamada, a very famous Japanese potter, uses only three basic glazes, one of which is a commercially produced clear glaze.

At stoneware temperatures, the body and glaze react together to form a strong bond and the body or slip has a powerful effect on the glaze. This can be illustrated quite simply by testing stoneware glazes over different coloured slips and comparing the results.

Tin oxide in amounts from six to twelve per cent will opacify clear glaze: amounts of ball or china clay will render it less shiny and may induce mattness. An excess of whiting will produce a stony matt finish, while additions of talc may give an opaque silky surface. Oxides can be used in the way indicated on the chart on pages 116-7.

Art glazes listed in suppliers' catalogues in the stoneware range are usually restricted to those used by traditional stoneware potters. They usually include a temmoku glaze which is a black glaze with an iron content of between eight to twelve per cent which breaks rust brown on edges. Further additions of iron produce the 'kaki' glaze which resembles tea dust in appearance. Black matt manganese glazes are listed which are useful for more decorative ware. Celadon glazes only reveal their true colour, which is a soft transparent green, in a 'reduction' kiln. In an electric kiln they usually appear as a pale honey colour. A 'reduction' kiln is one in which the atmosphere is affected by the fuel used. A gas or solid fuel kiln will give 'reduction' while an electric kiln will not. A dolomite glaze usually has an opaque soft silky surface which is extremely attractive both for domestic and more decorative ware. All these glazes can be very useful for the potter. The way glazes are used is, finally, more important than the way they are made. Glaze quality and colour must relate to the pot and form one single unit.

Recipes

Lists of ingredients of various glazes have often, in the past, been jealously guarded secrets of individual potters. This tradition was well and truly broken by Bernard Leach who, in *A Potter's Book*, published a long list of glaze recipes. When the contents of glazes are known, any imbalance which arises can be easily adjusted. With prepared glazes however, this is more difficult as manufacturers do not give their glaze recipes. However, the main difficulty with recipes is that neither raw materials nor firing conditions are identical for any two potters and therefore recipes do not always give the stated results. Recipes provide a useful working basis and I include a short list which will act as a starting point for other discoveries.

Earthenware glaze recipes
All fire to 1080°C Cone HO1. Figures express proportions by weight

Clear

Lead bisilicate	83
White earthenware clay	17

Stoneware glaze recipes
All fire to 1250°C Cone H8

Basic Clear Glaze

Feldspar	40
China clay	20
Quartz	20
Whiting	20

Pale Honey		**Ash Glaze**	
Lead Bisilicate	83	Ash	45
Red earthenware clay	17	Feldspar	33
		Dolomite	22

White Opaque Vellum		**Smooth Ash Glaze**	
Lead Bisilicate	84	Ash	38
White earthenware clay	16	Feldspar	36
Zinc oxide	3	China clay	10
Rutile	5	Ball clay	8
Tin oxide	9	Quartz	8

White Opaque		**White Opaque Glaze**	
Lead Bisilicate	50	Feldspar	60
China clay	15	China clay	25
Feldspar	25	Whiting	25
Whiting	10		
Tin oxide	8		
Rutile	2		

Natural materials

Experiments with locally available or unusual materials often yield surprisingly successful results. For decorative ware at earthenware temperatures, such experiments are limited to the use of pieces of coloured glass obtained from broken bottles or, for more spectacular results with a greater colour range, off-cuts from stained glass windows. The glass is simply put on top of the raw glaze and fired in the glaze firing. Some glass will be found to retain its colour more than other glass, and some will craze or develop hairline cracks. For practical reasons, glass should be fired inside bowls or small ash trays to prevent it running or, if small pieces are used, it can be fired on top of commercially produced white tiles for decorative effects. Experiments will show which glass is more suitable and the sort of effects which can be achieved. Ordinary household borax can also be used at earthenware temperatures. It must be applied as a powder to a horizontal surface as it is soluble in water. A small pinch of copper

H

oxide added to the borax will give a rich colouring of green and blue.

At stoneware temperatures the range of materials available for such experiments is much wider. Any local clay or soil can be tested, first on its own and then in combination with some fluxing material such as dolomite. Perhaps the main source of such experiments, however, is the wood ash obtained from burning wood or grass. Any organic ash, except that obtained from coke or coal, is suitable: cigarette ash, if sufficient quantity can be collected, any mixed wood ash, or single wood ash. Ash is usually prepared first by washing it in three or four changes of water and then sieving it through an 80 mesh sieve. When dry, it is treated as any other raw glaze material.

A simple recipe which will give reliable results with most ashes is: equal parts of ash, ball clay and feldspar.

Glaze faults

The glaze and body must fit together satisfactorily if they are to stand up to wear and tear in use. When the balance between glaze and body is upset faults occur, which can sometimes be cured by simple remedies. All experiments should be done on a small scale to begin with and carried out accurately.

CRAZING occurs when the glaze contracts more than the body. Fine hair line cracks appear which are especially noticeable in a transparent glaze. Add quartz to the glaze in small amounts of two per cent at a time to remedy this.

SHELLING is when the glaze contracts less than the body and under compression, the glaze spits off at the rim or edges of handles. Increase the flux content, such as lead or frit, or reduced the quartz content of the glaze to correct this.

CHIPPING Pots which chip easily may have too brittle a body which may be caused by the presence of too much sand or by over-firing or underfiring the body.

CRAWLING of the glaze into lumps rather than remaining as a flat even coating is often due to the presence of boro-calcite. Sometimes due to high viscosity such as excess of tin oxide.

BUBBLING Glaze surfaces should generally be smooth and even. Cratered surfaces usually result from over-firing which causes some glazes to boil and bubble.

PIN-HOLING Usually glazes which are too viscous or under-fired.

MATT SURFACES on shiny glazes usually result from under-firing.

Colour in glazes

Colour in glazes is obtained by adding small quantities of oxides to the basic glaze. The amount required is usually calculated quite separately to the glaze and is expressed as a separate percentage of the total glaze. Most colouring oxides lower the melting point of the glaze slightly and if used in large amounts an equal amount of china clay should be added.

The final colour which develops depends on the basic composition of the glaze. For example, bright colours tend not to develop in glazes high in alumina, turquoise can only be obtained in an alkaline base glaze, while lead glazes can give especially rich iron browns and midnight blues. The following chart lists the common metal oxides and gives an indication of the colours at different temperature in different sorts of glazes.

COLOUR CHART

Oxide	Earthenware		Stoneware
	Lead Glaze	Leadless	Oxidising Fire
Chromium Oxide 1%—3%	In tin oxide glazes 2% will sometimes give pink. In low temperature alumina free glazes, gives red. With zinc gives brown	Opaque greens in small quantities. Low temperature soda glaze with 1% will give yellow	Opaque greens. In dolomite or talc glazes small quantities may give pink
Cobalt Oxide ½%—3%	Pale blue to midnight blue at all temperatures. In glazes containing tin oxide will give a speckled effect unless very finely ground. Sometimes goes purple in glazes high in magnesium		
Copper Oxide or Copper Carbonate 1%—4%	Soft apple green 2% Metallic black 5—7%	Turquoise blue 3%	1½% will give soft olive green
Crocus Martis 1%—5% form of Iron Oxide	Gives brown/yellows. Gives good chestnut brown on tin oxide		
Iron Oxide 2%—8%	Pale yellow to dark brown. Warm colours	Pale yellow to dark brown but cool colours on the whole	Pale yellow to black to khaki 2%—15%

Colour Chart

Oxide	Earthenware		Stoneware
	Lead Glaze	Leadless	Oxidising Fire
Manganese Oxide 2%—8%	Browns, Lowers temperature of glaze slightly	Purple or brown or plum colour	Browns. 50% manganese 50% red clay will give black pigment. On its own will give rich dark brown surface painted directly onto body
	Gives especially good browns when combined with iron oxides and violet when combined with cobalt oxide		
Nickel 1%—3%	Brownish greens	Browns	Browns. In glazes with high zinc content gives yellow or blue
	Fugitive colours on the whole. Best used to soften other major oxides		
Rutile (Impure form of iron oxide)	Yellow broken effect	Yellow/creams	Breaks surface of glaze. Small quantities with cobalt breaks colour and adds interest
	Makes glazes opaque depending on amount used		

All colours can be mixed together to produce softer or intermediate shades. Many of the oxides, when used alone, give crude colours, these generally benefit from being softened by being used in conjunction one with the other.

Glaze stains

Manufacturers prepare glaze stains which are added to the basic glaze in quantities from two to ten per cent depending on the depth of colour required. Any manufacturer's instructions for their use should be followed.

Mixing glazes

Amounts of glaze should be weighed according to the recipes and added to water. Oxides are usually added at this stage. The glaze is stirred with the hand until all the lumps are broken and then put two or three times through an 80 mesh sieve until it is of smooth consistency (figure 38). Care should be taken to ensure that no solid material is thrown away during the sieving.

The necessary glaze consistency varies from one glaze to the other. Generally it needs to be creamy rather than thin and watery. When the correct consistency has been found,

Figure 38 Sieving glaze or slip

a simple hydrometer can be used to record this. A wooden stick, weighted at one end, is put in the glaze and a mark is made on the stick showing the level of the glaze. This will enable future batches to be mixed correctly. If the mark is above the surface the glaze needs more water, if below the surface, water must be removed after the glaze has settled.

Between use, glaze materials settle leaving a layer of clean water at the top. Before use, the glaze must be thoroughly mixed up and, if lumpy, sieved. Well fitting lids prevent the water evaporating and keep out foreign bodies.

Applying glazes

Glazes are prepared in the form of liquids and are usually applied to the pot when it has been biscuit fired. Some glazes such as those containing a high proportion of clay, can be used as a slip and are applied to the pot before it is biscuit-fired. Such pottery, known as once-fired ware, is economical to make. However, it is more convenient to biscuit fire the pots first as they are easier to glaze and handle.

Glaze, like slip, can be applied in many different ways. The simplest, easiest and most effective method is dipping the pot in glaze. If the pot is to be glazed inside and out, and the walls are not too thin this can be done in a single operation. Hold the pot firmly on the rim or foot with the fingers of either one or both hands, whichever is more convenient, and plunge it sideways into the glaze. Hold it to prevent airlocks forming inside which would stop part of it being glazed. Leave pot in glaze for a second, moving it slightly, lift it out, invert it, gently shaking it to remove glaze drips. When the glaze has been absorbed leave the pot to dry before fettling it ready for the kiln.

Applying the glaze by pouring is necessary when there

Figure 39 Glazing a large pot

is only a small quantity, or when the pot is too large to dip comfortably. Glaze the inside of the pot first and allow this to dry before glazing the outside. Support the pot upside down on two triangular sticks over a bowl on a banding wheel (figure 39). Slowly revolve the wheel and pour the glaze down the sides of the pot. Alternatively, if the pot is small, hold it by the foot over a bowl and pour the glaze down the sides.

Glaze can be painted on pots provided care is used to obtain an even covering. It is a method which is not easy or quick to carry out but is useful if only small areas are to be covered.

Spraying glaze is a method which gives a regular even covering but requires complex equipment. The fine spray of glaze is dangerous if inhaled in large quantities and spraying must therefore be carried out in an extraction booth. Small areas, however, can be sprayed with a hand spray such as those used by graphic designers, or a spray can be improvised from a stiff toothbrush.

Trailing glaze with a slip trailer is a more decorative way of using glaze. Slightly thicker glaze needs to be used and it is easiest to trail on flat, rather than vertical surfaces though with practice this can be done. Commercially produced glazed white tiles are ideal for trailed decoration at earthenware temperature and extremely rich, jewel-like effects can be achieved by this method.

Fettling the glaze

Fettling is a term used by potters to describe the process of preparing either glaze or biscuit pots for the kiln. Finger marks must be touched in with glaze and gently rubbed over to ensure a smooth covering. Drips too, must be gently rubbed over.

Stoneware pots must have all the glaze removed from the foot. During the firing the glaze melts and any glaze on the foot in contact with the kiln shelf will cause it to stick. Glaze must be wiped off the foot and about $\frac{1}{10}$in up the wall with a sponge. This is much more easily prevented in the first place by waxing the foot with hot wax or emulsion resist. In stoneware firings, lids are fired in position on the pot and surfaces which come in contact must also be free from glaze.

Earthenware can be fired in two ways. The foot ring can be cleaned as for stoneware, or the pot can be glazed all over and fired on spurs. These are three cornered tripods of refractory clay which support the pot above the kiln itself. They stick to the glaze in the firing and are subsequently pulled off. The spur marks are then smoothed over with a carborundum stone. Stoneware, however, is always fired standing on the kiln shelf as the clay softens slightly during the firing and would warp if supported on stilts.

8

Decorating with Glaze

When the pot has been biscuit-fired and is ready for glazing there are many ways in which it can be decorated both before the glaze is applied and after. This decoration is mainly done with the various colouring oxides applied to the raw glaze.

Underglaze colours

Colouring oxides, as well as being used in the glaze can also be used on top of the glaze or underneath it. True underglaze decoration is painted or applied in some other way to the unfired pot or direct to the biscuit-fired pot before being glazed. In this process the decorated pot is dipped in the glaze and in doing so a small amount of oxide is washed off into the glaze which is slightly coloured as a result. Colours can also be painted on the raw glaze. This technique is often known as underglaze decoration though, strictly speaking, it is in-glaze decoration as it goes in, rather than under, the glaze.

Colours used underneath glazes tend to be softer and more subdued in appearance than those painted on the glaze. Under transparent glazes the colours tend to run and streak and this tendency can be used to great decorative effect.

Colours painted on a white opaque tin glaze tend to remain where painted and this is the most popular method of decorating on white glazes. It is this decorative technique, sometimes known as majolica, which was developed originally by the Arab potters in the Near East and subsequently brought to Europe via Spain and Italy. Because the raw glaze is very absorbent, the mixed pigment must be painted with a full brush in broad strokes. No rubbing out is possible and small strokes or a 'filling-in' technique can look indecisive and messy.

Almost any colouring oxides can be used for underglaze decoration though some are more easily managed than others. Chrome oxide, for example, if applied too thickly will form an unpleasant opaque matt surface. Cobalt oxide which is very powerful, needs only a small amount to give a good colour, while an excess of copper oxide will give a black metallic surface edged with green.

The effects of painted oxides on different glazes can be demonstrated by making a series of six test tiles. On three tiles paint oxides directly on the biscuit clay, cover one tile with a lead glaze, one with a leadless glaze and one with a white opaque glaze. Glaze the last three tiles with the three different types of glazes and paint the oxides on to the raw glazes. Compare the effects obtained. Most of these tests can be made in earthenware and stoneware except that lead glazes cannot be used at stoneware temperatures.

Most metal oxides will withstand stoneware temperatures though they will give a slightly different colour effect to that obtained at the lower temperature. Stoneware glazes on the whole tend to be more viscous and less fluid and oxides will remain more or less where they are painted.

Underglaze colours are mixed with water by grinding them either with a pestle and mortar or on a smooth-surfaced tile th a knife. Oxides are expensive and small quantities go a long way. Any mixture which dries out should be kept for re-use. Slightly softer effects can be obtained by mixing a small amount of glaze with the oxides.

Underglaze colours can be applied by painting or spraying, or by any other suitable method. When used on the raw glaze they are best applied a few minutes after glazing, when the glaze has been absorbed, but before it has dried out completely. If the glaze forms ' blebs ' when the oxide is painted on, the glaze is probably too dry. If the brush wipes off the glaze, then the glaze is too wet and must be allowed to dry out more.

Some pottery suppliers sell underglaze crayons; these are sticks of underglaze colours which are only suitable for use on biscuit as they are not soft enough to be used on raw glaze. They are convenient for simple geometrical patterns and for marking the bottom of individual pots with a reference number when this is necessary.

Underglaze stains

Many manufacturers supply specially prepared underglaze stains which can be used more or less like metal oxides. Underglaze stains need only be mixed with water as they often have a small amount of glaze embodied in them. Some underglaze colours withstand stoneware firing and most are reliable over a wide temperature range. All colours can be mixed together to produce intermediate shades.

Double glazing

Certain glazes melt at slightly different temperatures and this quality can be used to great effect by double glazing the pot. By simple resist methods, three effects can be obtained on a single pot from two glazes. To be effective, of the two glazes to be combined one must begin to melt at a temperature lower than the other and be different in quality and effect. Experiments with various glazes one over the other will give some interesting results which can often be incorporated with great richness of effect on such things as bowls.

Simple combinations of dark and light glazes, viscous and fluid glazes have possibilities. A blank transparent glaze, for instance, under a white opaque glaze, will melt before the white glaze, bubble through and break the surface with an irregular and pleasing pattern of rich colour.

Glazes which are to be used for double dipping need to be slightly thinner than those for normal use. The success of double-dipping depends on choosing the right moment when the first glaze has dried sufficiently to absorb another glaze but not so much that it will lift the bottom glaze off the pot and cause blebs. If this happens, then glaze must be washed off, the pot dried out, and re-glazed.

RESIST Double glazing can be more effective if certain areas are made to resist the second glaze. Hot wax is the most effective method and simple bands as well as more decorative designs are effective.

SGRAFFITO Glaze, like slip, can be scratched to reveal the body underneath. When fine lines are scratched in the glaze, sufficient glaze is often left to partially glaze and darken the body in a rich and varied way. Some glazes are best scratched before drying while others seem to work better after drying. Sgraffito designs can also be efficiently double dipped to give subtle and delicate effects. Designs painted in underglaze too, can be lightly scratched to show the glaze underneath and to add detail or enhance the pattern in general.

Decorating the glazed pot

When the pot has been glaze-fired, it can still be decorated by the variety of techniques. Most of the painted and transfer decoration on fine porcelain and china made by the pottery industry, for instance, is all applied after the pot has been glaze-fired. Gold and silver lustres too, are supplied at this stage.

Enamel or on-glaze decoration

On-glaze decoration is so called because it is literally applied on top of the glaze. The decoration is done by using enamels which are low temperature glazes industrially prepared in the form of a frit.

Enamels are supplied in powdered form and need to be mixed with a special on-glaze liquid medium before use. The medium is a sticky oil and gum mixture which makes the enamel stick to the smooth glaze before it is fired in the kiln. At the low temperatures, at which enamels melt, the range of bright colours available is wide and, as they have been prepared in fritted form, the colour of the enamel changes little in the firing. The potter, therefore, has a true palette from which to work. Manufacturers usually specify exactly the temperature to which the enamels must be fired. Any other firing will result in the enamel losing its colour. The recommended firing temperature is usually around 750°C or cone HO16. At this temperature the enamels melt and bond firmly to the glaze which is relatively unaffected at this temperature.

Enamels are mixed with the liquid oil medium with either a palette knife on a tile or with a pestle and mortar. Several layers of enamel may have to be applied before sufficient thickness is achieved, but each layer must be allowed to dry before the next is applied. Brushes must be cleaned in turpentine spirit before the enamel sets hard. Unfired enamel designs can be removed with turpentine spirit.

Sprayed decoration used in conjunction with paper resist can be an effective method of applying enamels.

Lustres

Metallic lustre decoration is applied to the glazed pot in much the same way as underglaze decoration, and is fired to the same temperature.

It is purchased, specially prepared, in liquid form for direct application. Thinning medium can be used if necessary. Again, brushes and utensils must be cleaned with turpentine. Metal lustres are available in a wide range of colours from silver, gold, green and blue to mother-of-pearl. Small or large areas can be painted with lustre but it is expensive to purchase and smaller areas with carefully drawn designs can be very effective. Some potters have used lustre on dark glazed stoneware pots with extremely rich results. Sgraffito decoration can be scratched through the painted lustre after it has dried.

Paper resist

Decoration which relies on areas resisting pigment can be effectively achieved with gummed paper or Sellotape. This is easily stuck into position on the fired glaze and removed when the decoration is complete.

Re-glazing

A fired glazed pot which for some reason is unsatisfactory can sometimes effectively be re-glazed and re-fired. Providing the first firing did not over-fire the glaze leaving it bubbled and pitted, and providing the shape is not too complex to handle comfortably, re-glazing can be successful. The process is fairly straightforward. Re-glazing is usually done with glaze much thicker than that used for normal glazing. The addition of some sort of siccative, such as gum arabic, to the glaze will also help it to adhere to the smooth fired surface. Heating the pot first with hot water, or standing it in a medium hot oven will cause the glaze to dry more quickly and remain in position on the pot.

9

Kilns and Firing

When your pots have been made and dried out they are then ' fired '. In this process the clay is slowly and evenly heated until it is glowing red hot. At this temperature, which is around 650°C, an irreversible chemical change takes place in the clay, which prevents it from disintegrating in water and instead makes it hard and porous. The higher the temperature the harder the pot becomes. What actually happens is a complex chemical change, which results in the particles of clay fusing together to form a hard mass. As the temperature increases, the more the clay fuses together until, if the temperature was sufficiently high, the clay would melt and become liquid. At earthenware temperature most clays remain slightly porous, but at stoneware temperature, most clays have become almost completely vitrified – non-porous with the particles bonded well together.

In parts of Nigeria today, pots are fired in a way similar to that used thousands of years ago. The women of the tribe make the pots and conduct the firing. They carefully pack the pots on a layer of wood and more wood is packed over the pots. The fire is lit very slowly. A covering of dense grass or leaves is finally laid over the fire to prevent draughts of cold air reaching the pots which would cause them to crack. Only low temperatures can be obtained by this firing method and

I

the fired pots are porous and fragile and are marked black and brown from the flames. The pots which are fired by this method must be made from clay containing a good proportion of opening material, such as sand or grog, to prevent them shattering in the bonfire. No glaze can be used.

Firing pots in a bonfire is a fascinating introduction to the final process of making pottery even though only limited results can be achieved. The sawdust firing method, though similar to firing in a bonfire is more easily controlled. Pots are packed in sawdust inside a container of some sort and the sawdust is lit from the top (figure 40). A biscuit tin with small holes punctured in the sides, and a layer of coke in the bottom is a useful container. The pots need to be packed in between layers of well compressed sawdust with the largest pots at the bottom. As the fire burns slowly down, the pots are fired, though again the temperature which can be reached is quite low. Peat, if it is available, can also be

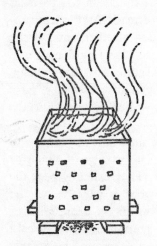

Figure 40 Sawdust firing in a biscuit tin

Figure 41 Small electric kiln

used instead of sawdust but must be set alight at the bottom and the pots packed on top of this. Both these firings will take twelve hours or more and need only sufficient draught to allow combustion to take place slowly.

Kilns

Various sorts of manufactured kilns can be bought, each type fired by a different sort of fuel which includes gas (town and natural), oil, wood and electricity. Of these types the easiest to install, the simplest to operate and cheapest to buy are worked by electricity and these kilns are the ones with which I am going to deal.

Electric kilns have basically a simple construction which consists of a well insulated box made of special refractory material which does not conduct heat. Round the walls of the box, inside special housings, are the electric heating elements probably in the form of wire coils (figure 41). A side door or a top lid enables the kiln to be packed. In the door there is usually a spy hole about $1\frac{1}{2}$in diameter, fitted with a clay bung. The inside of the kiln can be seen during the firing through the spy-hole. On the top of the kiln there is usually a vent, fitted with a removable brick or flap of some sort. The vent enables fumes to escape at the beginning of the firing and it allows the cooling process to be speeded up at the end of the firing.

As I said earlier, kilns must be heated slowly and the sudden switching on to maximum power of a kiln full of pots can cause the temperature to rise too quickly resulting in exploding pots. Some form of heat control is, therefore, fitted to most kilns. Temperatures in very small kilns can be built up by switching the kiln on and off for a few minutes which, though tedious, does work. Some kilns, however, are fitted with a simmerstat with a low, medium, high switch which puts on fewer or more of the elements at one time. The most sophisticated control is in the form of a heat input regulator. This is a finely-adjusted automatic switching device controlled by a manually operated dial numbered from 1–100. At a hundred the control is on full, at other times it puts the kiln on a percentage of the time. A setting of 50, for example, puts the kiln on and off for equal lengths of time which are approximately 50 seconds. The main advantage of heat input regulators is that all the elements are switched on or off by the mechanism and the heat is built up evenly through the kiln.

Temperature indicators
Temperatures inside the kiln can be measured in several ways. The simplest method is to look at the colour through the spy-hole. At 600°C a dark dull glow is seen which gradually gets brighter until around 900°C it appears to be a bright cherry colour. At 1100°C the colour is orange and at 1280°C a light lemon colour.

Experienced potters can recognize the temperature from the colour in the kiln. At temperatures over 1200°C the inside of the kiln is very bright and it is necessary to wear blue-tinted or dark glasses. Removing the bung from the spy-hole may also cause a stream of very hot air to come out of the kiln which will singe hair and eyebrows very quickly. Take care when looking inside your kiln and approach the spy-hole from below rather than above.

CONES Most of us need something more infallible than colour alone, and the commonest heat indicators are called cones. These are purchased ready-made and put inside the kiln, in front of the spy-hole. Cones are made from finely blended glaze materials in the form of tall three-sided tapering pyramids. The ingredients are carefully calculated to cause the cone to melt and fall over at a stated temperature. The have a number on them indicating the temperature at which they melt (figure 42). See chart for full details.

Staffordshire Cones (supplied by Podmore & Sons Ltd)

Cone Number	Temperature at which cones squat	
	°C	°F
H018	710	1310
H017	730	1346
H016	750	1382
H015	790	1454
H014	815	1499
H010	900	1652
H09	920	1688
H08	940	1724
H07	960	1786
H06	980	1796
H05	1000	1832
H04	1020	1868
H03	1040	1904
H02	1060	1940
H01	1080	1976
H1	1100	2012
H2	1120	2048
H3	1140	2084
H4	1160	2120
H5	1180	2156
H6	1200	2192
H7	1230	2246
H8	1250	2282
H8A	1260	2300
H8B	1270	2320
H9	1280	2336
H10	1300	2372
H11	1320	2408
H12	1350	2462

Cones are commonly sold in two sizes, standard $2\frac{5}{8}$in long, and miniature 1in long. The latter are useful for small spaces or when the spy-hole is very small.

Figure 42 Cones a Cones supported in clay before stoneware firing
b Cones after stoneware firing

Small stands made out of refractory clay can be bought to support the cones inside the kiln but are an unnecessary expense as a coil of clay wrapped round the base of the cone will do this quite efficiently. It is usual to put two cones in earthenware firing, one registering the temperature immediately below that required. In stoneware firings, three cones are often used, the two extra cones being those immediately below and above the required temperature. High temperatures take longer to spread evenly throughout the kiln and when the third cone begins to move over, the temperature should have become even throughout the kiln.

PYROMETERS More sophisticated heat-indicators are pyrometers. These are delicately balanced mechanisms and consist of a thermocouple fitted inside a porcelain sheath placed in position inside the kiln. This is connected by a cable to a pointer on a dial marked in degrees centigrade. The temperature inside the kiln is continually recorded by the instrument which is operated by expanding metal contacts. Visual temperature indicators such as these are, perhaps, the most useful, if the most expensive. They enable regular checks to be made to ensure that the temperature is rising at the correct speed and indicate the precise temperature at which to end the firing.

It is worth pointing out, however, that pyrometers do not always show the same temperature as corresponding cones; this is because pyrometers are sometimes calibrated slightly higher and because pyrometers measure the temperature of the kiln atmosphere and do not record, like cones, the effect of the heat. This difference is unimportant as long as it is taken into account in the firing and the use of the same method will ensure that similar results are obtained.

Firing temperatures

°C	Colour	Cone Number	Notes
650	Dark dull red		Clay irreversibly changed
750	Medium dark red	HO16	Enamels and lustres
980	Dark orange	HO6	Average biscuit temperature for studio ware
1080	Orange	HO1	Average earthenware temperature
1160	Pale orange	H4	Limit of most red earthenware clays
1250	Yellow	H8	Average stoneware temperature
1280	Pale yellow	H9	High stoneware temperature

Ancillary equipment

Kiln manufacturers state quite clearly in their catalogues what equipment is fitted to, and supplied with, their kilns. A pyrometer is not usually supplied with the kiln but is an extra which has to be paid for separately. There are various other mechanisms which can be fitted to the kiln to control the temperature rise. Some mechanisms eliminate the risk of over-firing and regulate the firing time as required.

Choosing a kiln

Large kiln manufacturers supply products which are for the

most part reliable and safe. Kilns of a similar size which cost more are often more robustly built. The catalogues of the three manufacturers listed on page 167 should cover the available range. Before making your choice try and estimate your needs as far as the size of the kiln, the space available in which the kiln is to fit and the cost and buying and installation are concerned.

Installation if kilns can be an expensive business if the existing power supply is inadequate. Check on this with your local electricity board. Kilns which can be operated with a 13 amp plug are usually too small for most potters, but are more suitable for enamelling and jewellery. A small sized kiln needs about as much power as an electric cooker, while a larger kiln (see kiln chart for full details) possibly requires the installation of special wiring. While electric kilns are perfectly safe in operation providing all the instructions are followed, they should be installed by a professional electrician as wiring which is overloaded can be dangerous and can also cause fires.

The size of the kiln is also determined by the amount of space which is available. For instance, even a small kiln will make an average size room quite hot and these sorts of considerations have to be taken into account. Kilns should be stood on a strong floor, preferably not wooden, and sufficient space left between the wall and the kiln – a foot is minimum, body space is better. The ceiling too, should be sufficiently high to be unaffected by the heat and, if in doubt, can be covered with a sheet of asbestos stocked by builders' merchants.

Manufacturers always specify the maximum temperature to which their kilns can safely be fired. This they determine by the quality and thickness of the construction and the type of heating elements installed. Electric heating elements are

KILN GUIDE

Description	Internal dimensions						Rating KW	Weight cwts	Cost (approx)
	height		width		depth				
Small	12in	x	9in	x	12in		3	3	£50
Medium	13in	x	12in	x	12in		4	3	
	16in	x	15in	x	15in		6	$5\frac{1}{4}$	£180
Good	19in	x	18in	x	18in		$9\frac{1}{2}$	$7\frac{1}{4}$	
useful size	19in	x	18in	x	24in		12	$7\frac{3}{4}$	
Large	25in	x	24in	x	24in		19	18	
	37in	x	24in	x	24in		23	25	£350
	43in	x	24in	x	36in		32	39	

Kilns supplied by Podmore & Sons Ltd

made from a high temperature metal alloy and the ' Kanthal ' type is the most common. Ordinary Kanthal wire will fire to 1200°C while Kanthal A1 will fire to 1300°C. The initial difference in cost between high temperature and low temperature kilns similar in size is very small. Is it usually worth getting the high temperature kiln even if only earthenware firings are originally planned.

Kiln care

With use, bits of clay and dust will settle in the element housing, and in the corners of the kiln. These can be carefully removed with a fine brush or vacuum cleaner. After use metal heating elements become very brittle and should not be moved or touched with glaze. If glaze is accidentally knocked onto the element it should be gently brushed off. When elements burn out, all traces of the old element should be chiselled out of the kiln wall before a new element is put in.

Kiln furniture

The inside of kilns have no permanently fixed furniture or fittings so that shelves can be put in position in each firing with regard to the height of the pots. New kilns are usually supplied with the necessary kiln furniture, which consists of shelves and props. These are either designed for use at low temperatures or for high temperatures. If ordering extra shelves or props, higher temperatures ones are stronger. Shelves vary in thickness according to their span and the temperature at which they have to be fired. Larger shelves are thicker. Shelves which have warped have only a limited use and can be disastrous in stoneware firing by causing the pots to distort when the clay softens slightly.

Two sorts of props are commonly made (figure 43). One sort which consists of plain hollow cylinders of various lengths, are perhaps most useful. The other sort are castellated so they fit firmly together. Eventually they stick under pressure of heat and weight and are best avoided.

Shelves need to be painted with a layer of batt wash before

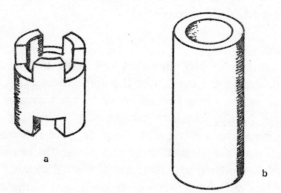

Figure 43 Props   a Castellated props   b Cylindrical props

use. This is made by mixing two parts quartz, two parts china clay and one part fine zircon sand. Batt wash prevents pots sticking to the kiln shelf and it also helps to prevent any glaze which runs down the pot bonding to the shelf. After each firing the shelves should be checked for cracks and any bits of pot or glaze removed by rubbing with a carborundum stone or a wire brush. Props too, should be similarly checked.

Biscuit firing

The first firing, which changes the clay into porous pottery, is usually known as the biscuit or bisque firing. Biscuit pots can be packed inside or on top of each other providing the weight is evenly distributed and providing that the clay can first expand with the heat and then contract as the temperature affects the chemical composition of the clay. Kiln packs should be as tight and economical as possible with a minimum amount of kiln furniture being used.

All pots must be absolutely dry before being put in the kiln. Dry pots tend to show a lighter colour at the edges, though this is not an infallible guide. The clay also comes away as powder if scratched. Generally, pots need a week in a warm dry atmosphere to dry out completely. Pots explode or crack because of steam rather than air bubbles trapped in clay.

Before being packed in the kiln each pot should be carefully examined for cracks or bits of clay and, if necessary, cleaned. If rough, the base of the pot should be smoothed over with fine wire wool or a fine damp sponge. The inside should also be checked to ensure that no bits of clay are present. Handle and spout joints often need to be checked and smoothed over.

Pots can be packed in the kiln rim to rim and base to

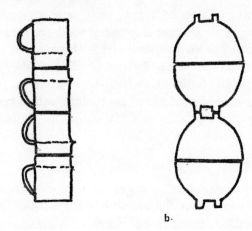

Figure 44 Packing pots in the biscuit firing   a Mugs can be packed rim to rim   b Bowls rim to rim

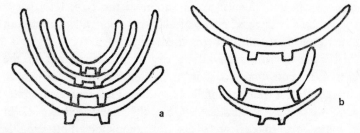

Figure 45 Stacking bowls one inside the other   a Correct – foot rims supported firmly one above the other   b Incorrect – weight not evenly distributed

base to quite a good height (figure 44), but pots must not be pushed along the shelf as they chip easily. Bowls can be packed inside each other providing the foot sits firm and the sides do not touch (figure 45). A space of about 1in should be left between the pots and the kiln walls to allow the air to circulate round the kiln.

In both biscuit and glaze firings, shelves should be stood

on three rather than four props. This prevents wobbling as well as being more economical to fire.

The cone – only one is necessary for a biscuit firing – should be placed inside the front of the spy-hole and an electric torch can be used to check that it is in position. Ensure that the cone can bend over without falling on any pots. Most studio biscuit is fired at 980°C which leaves the pot sufficiently porous to absorb glaze.

It is also possible to make grog or calcine materials such as clay in the biscuit firing. Powdered clay fired inside pots will make a fine grog at biscuit temperature.

Biscuit firings must start very slowly with all vents open to allow moisture to escape and so prevent explosions. On simmerstat control low is sufficient, on heat-input control 15 is safe. The temperature rise should be slow at this stage and takes about four hours to reach 200°C in a medium sized kiln. After this it can be speeded up with controls turned to medium, but with the vent still open. At 600°C vent can be closed and controls turned up to full until 980°C is reached. The total firing time will depend on the size of the kiln and the amount of pottery it contains, so no hard and fast rules can be made. Thick-walled and large pots need a slower firing than small thin-walled pots.

There is usually no need to soak a biscuit kiln (that is, maintain the maximum temperature for a while). However, if the clay contains a large amount of vegetable matter an hour's soak will be needed around 800°C, with the top vent open and the control turned down to maintain, but not increase, the temperature. This will enable any vegetable matter to burn away. Pale blue fumes usually indicate the need for such a soak.

Switch the kiln off as soon as the required temperature has been reached. Allow the kiln to cool slowly until 200°C at which point the vent can safely be opened. At 100°C the door can be opened slightly and the kiln unpacked when the pots are cool enough to handle. Generally speaking, a kiln takes the same time to cool as it does to heat up.

Check all pots as they are taken out of the kiln and remove any dust with a stiff brush before they are glazed. Any fine small cracks can be filled with biscuit stopper pushed lightly into the crack or split, with the edge of a knife. Biscuit stopper is a mixture of waterglass and fine red grog.

Biscuit Firing Chart

Temperature °C	Control	Vent	Effect
0—200	Low	Open	Steam evaporates
200—600	Medium	Open	Irreversible change in clay
600—800	Top	Closed	Body further hardened
800	Medium	Open	Burn away all carbon and sulphur
800—900	Top	Closed	Harden body further

Glaze firing

Unlike biscuit pots, glazed pots must not be allowed to touch each other in the kiln nor must any glazed part of the pot come into contact with either the kiln wall or the kiln shelf. Packing a glaze firing is, therefore, a much longer and more tedious process in which great care must be taken to see that the glaze is not damaged at all. Some raw glazes are very powdery and easily rubbed off. Glaze on rims is also very fragile and, if knocked, chips off easily. Pigment painted on glaze is easily smudged and must therefore be handled as little as possible.

Industrial earthenware is glazed all over and stood on stilts in the kiln. This method of firing is made possible by the use of thinly applied glaze which does not run into the firing. These conditions, however, for the studio potter are too difficult to achieve. Instead, the studio potter usually leaves the foot ring and a small part up the side of the pot unglazed, to prevent any glaze running on to the kiln shelf. The pot is then placed directly on the kiln shelf.

Fettling glazed ware involves checking each pot to see that no glaze has been rubbed off or chipped. The foot and bottom of the walls must be checked to ensure that they are free from glaze. Lidded stoneware pots must have the edges and housing of the lids checked to ensure that no glaze is present and the lid is correctly in position. When a stoneware body which softens considerably in the firing has been used, it is often necessary to paint a wash of sand and batt wash in the lid housing to ensure the lid does not stick to the pot.

It is useful to keep small jars of glaze near the kiln to touch up any chipped or rubbed glaze when the pot is being packed. This makes constant journeys to and from large glaze buckets unnecessary, as well as being much more easily mixed than buckets of glaze. Different raw glazes tend to look alike on pots, and it is often useful to write the glaze reference number onto the surface of the pot with a soft lead pencil. Alternatively, vegetable ink, which burns away in the kiln, can be used.

Just as biscuit kilns need packing economically, so do glaze kilns though this is more difficult. It can, however, be made simpler by initially sorting out pots of the same height which can be put on the same kiln shelf. Very small pots can often be placed in between large pots. Test tiles and such like can be fitted in last. Shelves and props which have become worn sometimes sit unevenly. This can be remedied in two ways. Sand placed underneath the props will sometimes be sufficient or thin flat pads of fireclay, dipped in sand, will act as suitable levellers. There are no hard and fast rules for packing successful glaze firing except that if there is any doubt about space it is best to leave the pot out.

Finally the cones should be placed in position behind the spy-hole. They should be placed so that the number on the cones can be seen. Place the cones a few inches back inside the kiln so that they are not affected by the cold spot which usually forms in front of the spy-hole.

Firing faults

'Kissing' is a fault of over-packing and occurs when pots are placed too close together and the glazes stick. Another common fault is 'tender-edges', in which the edges of the foot ring stick to the kiln shelf. The remedy lies in applying a thin wash of sand to the foot of the pot. 'Dunting' is a fault in which the pots crack and is often due to too rapid kiln cooling. Other firing faults such as bloating and squatting are usually due to over-firing rather than bad kiln packing.

Firing the kiln

Glaze firings can be done much faster than biscuit firings as many of the changes in the clay have already been made. The firing should still begin cautiously and can gradually be speeded up until a suitable firing schedule has been worked out. A change in the clay again occurs around 570°C and the temperature increase should not be fierce at this point or cracking may occur. Some potters end their stoneware firings by soaking for up to an hour. Whether you decided to soak or not is a matter of individual choice. If glazes are smoother or more preferable when they have been soaked then, soak, if no different, then no soak is necessary. Earthenware glazes rarely, if ever, need soaking. Check the kiln every thirty minutes until the end of the firing when fifteen minute and

Glaze Firing Chart			
Temperature °C	Control	Vent	Effect
0—200	Medium	Open	Steam evaporates
200—600	Medium	Open	Chemical change in clay repeated
600	Full	Closed	
1080	Earthen-ware	Closed	
1250	Stoneware	Closed	Soak at maximum
1250	Medium	Closed	temperature if necessary
1250	Off	Closed	

finally five-minute intervals are necessary. When a firing schedule has been worked out, early checks can be made less frequently.

Unpacking the kiln

Allow the kiln to cool down slowly and open the door when the pots can be handled – which is a temperature below 100°C. However impatient you are to see the results of your work – and I for one am very impatient – resist the temptation until no damage will come to your work by too rapid cooling.

Check each pot as it is taken from the kiln and rub the base with a carborundum stone to remove any sand or glaze. Do not run your fingers round the base until it has been smoothed over as small pieces of glaze have razor sharp edges. Clean shelves and props and check to see that all elements are working.

Enamels and lustres

Enamels and lustres, mixed with on-glaze medium, must be fired in a well ventilated kiln until 400°C when all the oil has burnt away. If this does not take place in a clean atmosphere the colours lose their brilliance and the vapour settles on the

K

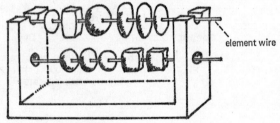

Figure 46 Support for beads

elements which damages them. The kiln can be ventilated by leaving the door open slightly and this must obviously be done with care. Kilns which have doors fitted with cut-out switches can sometimes be adjusted to work with the door open. Ensure that the enamels are not over fired as this causes loss of colour. Pack the enamel kiln as for an ordinary glaze firing, with no pots touching.

Firing beads
Beads which are glazed all over cannot be stood directly on top of the kiln shelf, they must be threaded on to element wire which is supported on a suitable stand made out of fire clay (figure 46). Kanthal A wire is able to withstand the heat better than ordinary element wire, but the total weight of beads should be limited otherwise they cause the wire to sag in the kiln.

10

The Workshop

With a little experience it will soon become obvious that some sort of workshop is necessary. While many pottery techniques can be adequately carried out on the kitchen table, the continual business of clearing away and storing work will begin to seriously threaten the activity. Clay can be a messy material which, like dust, can seem to permeate the whole house, and it is best not to forget this. In Chapter 1 I mentioned briefly the care necessary in keeping a workshop clean and tidy. In this chapter I will discuss ways of organizing a small pottery together with all the necessary equipment and lists of supplies.

A pottery is ideally situated in a separate building preferably adjacent to your house. A shed or outbuilding of reasonable size fitted with a suitable electricity and water supply would satisfy most potters. An inside room in the house can easily be turned into a workshop providing the floor is kept clean by washing and a clean, stiff mat is used to prevent clay being carried about on shoes.

If the room in which you are going to work is sufficiently large the kiln can be installed in it. This is an excellent arrangement as all activity takes place together which can result in a linking together of the making and firing processes in a helpful and constructive way. It also helps to eliminate the tiring and tedious moving of work from one room to the other.

A small electric kiln installed in a workshop will, when in operation, give off a large amount of heat and while this can be extremely pleasant in the winter months it can be uncomfortable in the summer. Some clays also give off fumes during the firing and these need to be removed by some form of ventilation. A powerful extractor fan fitted in the window will often do this efficiently and will keep the air circulating.

The way you plan the arrangement of your workshop will be determined by the space available, but as a general rule similar processes should be kept together in one area. The three basic activities – making pots, preparing and applying glazes, and firing – are processes which can be usefully separated, either in the same room or in quite separate areas.

Damp cupboard

The amount of heat generated by the kiln poses a problem as far as drying pottery is concerned. A dry warm atmosphere will, of course, cause clay and pots to dry very rapidly and some sort of cupboard will be necessary in which pots can be kept damp. Old coal cellars are ideal for this purpose but a damp cupboard can be improvised from any stoutly built cupboard or chest. The sides and door should be lined on the inside with polythene sheets firmly tacked or stapled in position. The shelves should be slatted rather than solid and be adjustable in height to accommodate pots of different sizes. On the floor of the cupboard a block of plaster of Paris or builders' red bricks continually soaked with water will help to keep the inside damp and prevent the pots drying out rapidly. Pots, however, have a habit of drying out even in what appear to be highly efficient damp cupboards. Occasionally extra precautions can be taken such as wrapping individual pots in sheets of polythene or covering freshly thrown pots with an inverted biscuit tin, before putting them into the damp cupboard.

Clay is stored ideally in a cool damp room of some sort. When this is not possible it can, if wrapped securely in sheets of polythene, be kept outside on the coolest side of the house. In winter, however, remember that frozen clay is not much use until it has thawed out. The working qualities of clay improve with keeping and, if space is available, the longer it is stored, the better is becomes. Six months to a year would be considered, by many potters, to be ideal.

Shelves

It is amazing how quickly work accumulates in the pottery. A look around many studios will reveal quantities of work started but not finished, ideas uncompleted, remains of orders and so on. Good, strong shelves are therefore essential if your working space is to be kept free. Shelves can be quickly and firmly built with the use of slotted angle iron made by Dexion Ltd. Shelves reserved for particular sorts of ware will provide a regular basis to the organization of your workshop. For example, shelves near the kiln, kept specially for biscuit and glazed ware, will help to ensure that no pots are overlooked when the kiln is being packed. Avoid placing inflammable material, such as wood, near the kiln, though it is obviously useful to use the space above the kiln. Permanent wooden shelves are a fire risk best avoided. On the other hand, a framework of metal supports on which shelves could be placed temporarily, would be useful for drying out pots or clay.

An alternative to using 'Dexion' for wall shelves is to make wooden supports with holes for pegs which can support removable shelves (figure 47). The basic wooden supports,

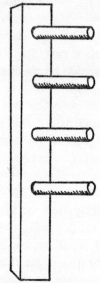

Figure 47 Peg support for shelves

about 3in wide and 2in deep, drilled with $\frac{5}{8}$in holes for the pegs, are secured firmly into position. Pegs about 8in long will be held firmly in position by the holes and support shelves 6in wide and about 4ft long. Shelves are ideally made from non-warping well seasoned pine, if available.

Apart from personal choice as to the planning of shelves, it is helpful to remember that buckets of glaze and slip are often more safely stored out of the way if stood on a wide shelf. In general, the more shelves the better.

Tables and wedging-bench

A strong wooden table makes an excellent work bench. An old fashioned kitchen table, for example, would be ideal. So is a woodworker's bench which has the added advantage of extra weight. Wooden surfaces are nicest to work on but Formica gives a pleasant, easily cleaned surface. At some point a perfectly flat surface, for rolling out clay or building slab pots, will be necessary, and this is often best provided by an old drawing board or piece of thick non-warping plywood. Marble slabs from the tops of old wash-stands also fulfil this task excellently.

Buckets and bins
All buckets and bowls are ideally made out of plastic which is quieter in use and easier on the hands. Well fitting lids help to prevent liquids drying out and keep out dust and bits of clay.

Wheel
So far I have looked at all the basic equipment involved in establishing a workshop except for the choice of wheel. These can either be bought, or built according to plans obtained from the addresses listed on page 165. Manufactured wheels vary considerably in price and efficiency. The easiest to work are electrically operated and the most expensive wheels – such as those supplied by either Podmores or Wengers – are over £100. These wheels are, however, strong and provide low speeds without loss of strength. The speed adjustment is delicate and altogether the wheels are very efficient. Other, less expensive, electric wheels tend to be excellent for work at higher speeds but poor at providing slow even speeds, which makes certain throwing tasks very difficult.

Wheels which are manually operated by kicking a bar or pedal with your foot again fall into two types. The Leach wheel which costs around £50 to buy is operated from a sitting position and, while it restricts the amount of clay which can be thrown at any one time, is in all other respects ideal. It responds rapidly to changes in speed and allows sensitive control of the throwing process. Of course, it does require that the knack of kicking and throwing be learned, and at first, the operation of the wheel is very tiring. The other type of common kick-wheel is operated by kicking a bar under the wheel from a standing position. These wheels are extremely difficult to operate efficiently and even skilled potters find them almost impossible to use. While they have a certain use for turning or the technique of coiling and throwing, they are not recommended for the potter who seriously wants to learn to throw.

Small equipment

It is possible to improvise many of the small pieces of equipment which are necessary in the pottery. Naturally, the list varies from potter to potter but there is a basic list which is useful as a guide. Much of this equipment can be ordered from the large firms but often at inflated prices. While, in terms of convenience, it is useful to order equipment from a catalogue, most hardware shops, or ironmongers or builders' merchants, will prove a suitable and less expensive source. The kitchen, too, is often a good source of interesting and useful tools.

POT SUPPORTS Coil pots or thrown pots need to be kept on some sort of support. Tiles, wood or asbestos are suitable. Builders' merchants sell large sheets of asbestos in various grades and thicknesses and this can be broken into small pieces by scoring a line with a pointed tool such as a bradawl or screwdriver. It can also be made into batts for use on the wheel though as these are not round, care has to be taken when using them. Specially made round wheel batts can be purchased made out of either asbestos or marine plywood.

SCALES Large scales, for weighing out glaze materials, like those used in greengrocers, can be purchased from kitchen suppliers or, sometimes, second-hand suppliers. It is more difficult to obtain fine scales for weighing out small test quantities. Delicate chemical balances, while ideal, are slow to use and extremely expensive to buy. Some photographic shops sometimes have second-hand though less ornate balances, for sale. Boxes of smaller metric weights are also sold here, and it is often worth trying such shops. The recent vogue for almost anything antique has caused prices of old fashioned objects to rise but some antique shops may have suitable balances for sale at reasonable prices.

CONES Cones must be bought from pottery suppliers and cost approximately £1.25 per 100 or 2p each. The temperature at which you are going to fire your pottery will determine which cones you want. A detailed chart is on page 133.

SIEVES Most kitchens are equipped with sieves, some with fairly fine mesh. Specially made sieves are supplied by the pottery manufacturers and, while they are fairly expensive to buy, they are vital for the production of smooth slips and glazes. Apart from stating the diameter of the sieves, the mesh grade is also included and this refers to the number of holes per square inch. A 40 mesh is therefore fairly coarse and a 120 mesh is fine. For most purposes an 80 mesh sieve of 10in diameter is quite adequate. Some glazes are improved by being put through 120 mesh but this is not essential for most glazes. For the initial sieving of coarse materials such as wood ash, household sieves can be used, followed by the 80 mesh sieve. This task will be made easier if plenty of water is used.

Small test sieves can be purchased and are a useful invest-ment. Made out of either tin or plastic material about 3in in diameter, they are ideal for sieving tests – even those as low as 2oz. Test sieves can easily be made if soldering equipment is available. The necessary mesh can be fixed to the bottom of a used tin or similar receptacle.

PESTLE AND MORTAR A second-hand pestle and mortar is worth searching for as new ones are expensive, but one can be bought from the suppliers.

BRUSHES (figure 48) Just as a painter prefers special brushes for certain jobs, so too does the potter. A recent visit to an army surplus store resulted in the purchase of several cheap and useful brushes. Of those the most useful has proved to be the shaving-brushes sold at $2\frac{1}{2}$p each, which are ideal for sieving or mixing small quantities of glaze. Large brushes with stiff bristles simplify the process of sieving by helping to break up any lumps and push them through the sieve.

Glaze mops have large full soft hair and, though expensive to buy, are ideal for blobbing on glaze or slip. Flat Japanese brushes with soft hair are even more expensive but again beautiful to work with.

For painting on pigment or underglaze colours most potters prefer Japanese brushes. These are now imported into this country in large quantities and while they are not cheap – especially the large full ones which are very expensive – they are a pleasure to handle and use.

ROLLING GUIDES AND ROLLING PINS A strong rolling pin about 16in long preferably without handles is ideal. Wooden rolling guides can usually be improvised. The neces-sary thickness will of course depend on individual require-

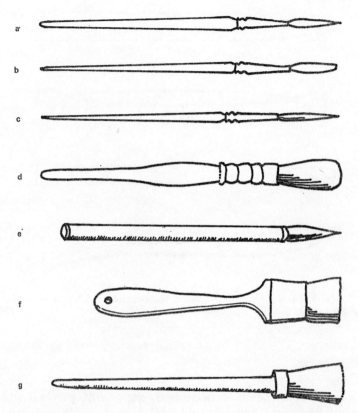

Figure 48 Different types of brushes   a Cut-liner for painting fine lines
b Flat ended 'liner' for painted decoration   c Long haired paint brush
for detailed decoration   d Soft haired glaze mop for touching up glazed
pots   e Long haired Japanese brush for brushwork   f Flat, soft haired
brush for large areas   g Stiff bristled sieving brush

ments, but guides $\frac{3}{8}$in and $\frac{5}{8}$in thick will prove useful.

WIRE   Almost any type of wire can be used providing it is
flexible and strong. Nylon thread can also be used. The

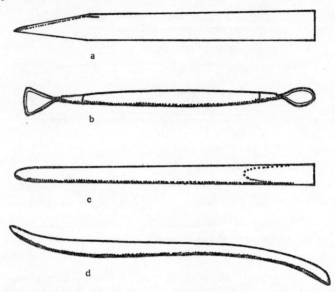

Figure 49 Wooden modelling tools   a Pointed tool   b Loop ended tool
c Flat ended tool   d   Curved tool

Craftsmen Potters Association sell excellent wire in varying thicknesses.

TOOLS   Any selection of tools is, necessarily, personal and depends on the type of work and individual requirements. An old-fashioned knife and fork box makes an excellent small tool store. A wide variety of boxwood tools are supplied by many manufacturers and, though not cheap to buy, are, as well as being useful, pleasant to handle (figure 49). A porcupine quill or a needle fastened in the end of a cork will suffice for trimming the tops of pots. Hacksaw blades broken into short strips, screws, nails, pieces of ruler, cogs, forks, a variety of kitchen and pocket knives are all useful. A carborundum stone and a wire brush, both available from ironmongers are also useful. Deck-chair canvas and flat pieces of hessian for rolling out clay on, can be acquired. A ruler, set-square and compasses will complete the personal tool-kit.

SPONGES   Two sorts are required. Large synthetic sponges for wiping brushes and mopping up generally are best bought locally. Fine small natural sponges for use on pots or during throwing can be purchased from chemists (large sponges can be cut up), or from the potters' suppliers.

SLIP TRAILERS   Enema syringes obtainable from chemists are perhaps the best and are suitable for both slip and glaze, though almost any collapsible plastic bottle fitted with a nozzle – such as those pieces of rubber used on the inside of tyre valves – can be improvised.

Materials

Clay

The basic material – clay – is all you need to start making pots. This, as explained in Chapter 1, can be obtained from any local source or bought in powdered or plastic form from clay suppliers. The price of clay varies from about 75p to £2 a hundredweight, depending on the quality and quantity bought. Carriage can roughly be reckoned to cost as much as the clay on small quantities. It is important to decide, at the beginning, the temperature at which you are going to fire your pots, as this does have a bearing on the clay and other raw materials you buy. For earthenware use, I would recommend any red firing clay (Hamsey Brick Company's is one of the cheapest). For stoneware, Moira Pottery Company supply, at a reasonable price, an excellent clay which fires a buff colour. Local potteries will often sell the odd hundredweight of clay and may indeed prove a continuing reliable source.

Raw materials

Again, the price of raw materials varies according to the amount purchased. The larger the quantity bought, the cheaper it is sold. There is, however, little point in buying a hundredweight if all you need is a few pounds. Fourteen or twenty-one pounds are usual quantities to order and store. No raw materials, providing they are kept dry and clean, deteriorate with being stored. Some potters, including myself, like to empty raw materials into storage containers of some sort. The hessian, paper or plastic bags in which materials are delivered hold dust and are messy to use. Plastic dustbins which cost around £1.50 solve this problem very well.

The following list is a guide to the necessary basic materials. I have omitted some materials mentioned in the text because they are not absolutely necessary at first, but can be added as and when they are needed.

EARTHENWARE

21lb clear transparent earthenware glaze
2lb tin oxide
14lb lead bisilicate
14lb ball clay
7lb china clay
7lb quartz
7lb feldspar
7lb borax frit
14lb sand
7lb zircon sand

STONEWARE
21lb clear transparent stoneware glaze
2lb tin oxide
7lb borax frit
7lb ball clay
14lb china clay
14lb quartz
21lb feldspar
7lb whiting
7lb dolomite
7lb talc
14lb sand
7lb zircon sand

Metal oxides
To all intents and purposes metal oxides work well at either earthenware or stoneware temperature. I have listed the most useful oxides separately from those which can be included later.

METAL OXIDES
7lb iron oxide
7lb manganese oxide
2lb copper carbonate
1lb cobalt oxide
3lb rutile

CAN BE ADDED LATER
1lb chrome oxide
1lb nickel oxide
1lb crocus martus

What do I make?

This is a question we all ask ourselves from time to time and one for which there is no easy answer. A good starting point is often found by someone saying 'Oh well, what I need is . . .' and then listing such things as a large or small teapot, tiles, plates, etc. With this need as stimulation it is often possible to start work and design for a particular purpose.

Clay has the great advantage of being versatile. It can be formed into almost any shape, not only those traditionally made, and so you can make all those objects for which you have a use but which are not produced commercially. There is no reason, also, why almost every pot used in the kitchen or on the dining table should not be made by you.

Another start is often found by visiting shops selling studio pottery which are often good places in which to find 'ideas'. It is helpful to see what other potters are making and to look at their designs and the quality of their craftsmanship. Their work may also stimulate you to make similar or even better products. A list of such shops and galleries is:

Craftsmen Potters Association
William Blake House
Marshall Street London W1

Craft Centre of Great Britain
43 Earlham Street London WC2

Northern Craft Centre
35 South King Street
Manchester 2

Scottish Craft Centre
Acheson House
Canongate
Edinburgh Scotland

Midland Group Gallery
11 East Circus Street
Nottingham
(occasional exhibitions of pottery)

Form and function

A few notes on shape and function will perhaps help the
new potter. Form is, I think, the most important consideration
of all for the potter as it is the basis on which the success of
the work depends. Skilled making techniques, sensitive glazing
and expert firing will not enhance a bad or weak form while a
strong lively form will be undaunted by poor technique –
though that is not an excuse for careless craftsmanship. The
point is that form must be strong, clear and related to function. The latter I will deal with subsequently, the former,
however, is not as easy to discuss.

A study of some of the best modern pottery will reveal why
it is successful. The pots may, in fact, appear deceptively
simple, with the finished pot looking as if it had almost
happened on its own, so obvious does its unity seem. Yet
strong form and good style develop only with experience and
individual potters continue for years to explore and exploit
the range of forms they know and understand in an effort
to achieve even greater simplicity and clarity. This intensive
search into a limited range of materials and form gradually
brings some sort of understanding which is conveyed effort-
lessly in the pottery. Line and form and surface quality become

L

linked in a way which would have been impossible without considerable experience.

Some potters prefer to make forms which are variations of straight sided cylinders with the shape being articulated by strong lines or clear changes in direction. Other potters like the smooth pureness of gently swelling curved form, with one shape running smoothly into or out of the next. So the choices are made. Rarely does a potter make pots which are totally dissimilar to each other. What we all try to do is to find a direction along which we can work, and then pursue it, working out each step as we go along.

Functional ware

It is, in a way, easier to deal with the practical relation of shape and form to use rather than the more difficult question of aesthetic understanding of form. Most potters make domestic ware for use either in the kitchen or on the table. Such ware has to fulfil certain functions.

Cooking pots, for example, must not crack when placed in, or taken out of, the oven. The red-bodied ware, made in such countries as Spain and Portugal, for use in the direct flame are only possible because of the nature of the red clay which occurs there naturally. Such wares cannot be easily made in Britain. Pottery, which can be used in the oven is however, the nearest we can get to this. To give cooking pottery sufficient strength to withstand the sudden changes in temperature glazes and body must fit well together without crazing or shelling and the body must not be too dense or brittle. Handles and knobs should be large enough to hold when hot with a cloth and lids should fit well and firmly. The glaze surface should be smooth and allow for easy cleaning.

As far as decoration goes on pottery, the choice must again be personal, but I feel richly decorated pottery does not always show food off to its best advantage. After all, at a meal, it is the food which is to be delicious and not particularly the pottery.

Tableware, too, presents us with practical problems. For example cups should sit firmly in saucers which allow plenty of room for a spoon. Rims of cups should be smooth and a slightly flaring rim which is not too thick is more pleasant to drink from than one which is thick and turned inward. Teapots are perhaps the most advanced shapes from a technical point of view and present numerous functional as well as aesthetic problems. For example spouts must not be below the maximum possible water line, nor must they dribble when tea is poured. Holes at the base of the spout should let tea through but not tea leaves. The handles should provide a firm grip, as close to the pot as possible, without causing fingers to get burnt. And so the list goes on. While it is important to be aware of the problems – and listening to criticism can be helpful in this respect – experience will in most cases suggest some sort of solution.

Man has been making pottery for many thousands of years. While this accumulated wealth of knowledge cannot be acquired in a week or even a year – it is reckoned that it takes five years to become a fully trained potter – it is possible to learn much more from the experience of others. This book is a result of my experience as a potter and is a practical guide to the craft which, as well as explaining the basic techniques, is useful in suggesting lines of development. Begin by making any sort of pottery you feel capable of tackling covering as wide a range of techniques as possible. Draw on this experience to work out what sort of pottery you want to make, and limit your raw materials accordingly. Explore these fully, and discover the many possibilities available within this range before adding other materials. The resulting pottery has a way of rewarding and justifying such work. Above all, enjoy making pottery; it is a fascinating craft which has endless possibilities once the basic rules are learned. Be patient, and good luck.

Suppliers of Materials

Mellor Mineral Mills Ltd Etruria Vale Stoke-on-Trent	Clays, slips and matching glazes
Moira Pottery Co Ltd Moira Nr Burton-on-Trent	Clays and glazes
Podmore & Sons Ltd Shelton Stoke-on-Trent	General materials and equipment
Wengers Ltd Stoke-on-Trent ST4 7OQ	Materials and equipment
Pike Bros Pike Fayle & Co Ltd Wareham Dorset	Pikes No 4 ball clay (and other ball clays)
Watts, Blake & Bearne Co Ltd Park House Courtenay Park Newton Abbot Devon	Earthenware and stoneware bodies
Hamsey Brick Co Ltd South Chaily Nr Lewes Sussex	Throwable red burning clay 950–1200°C. Very cheap

Dexion Ltd
Dexion House Empire Way
Wembley Middx

Slotted angle iron

Bill & Vicki Read
Claycutters Studio
Sheep St Winslow Bucks

New Kasenit 18 Gas Kiln
Town, Natural or Propane
Gas

Technical Art Products
202 Turnpike Link
East Croydon Surrey

Liquid emulsion wax resist

Woodleys Joinery Works
Newton Poppleford Devon

New improved Leach kick-
wheels

Potclays Ltd
Wharf House Copeland Street
Hanley Stoke-on-Trent

Clays and slips

Craftsmen Potters Shop
William Blake House
Marshall Street London W1

Pots, pottery books and
potters' sundries at very
reasonable prices

Kiln and wheel plans

C.O.S.I.R.A.
35 Camp Road Wimbledon Common
London SW19
Supply plans for Leach type kick-wheels, oil, wood and coke
fired kilns of various sizes
Shell International Petroleum Co Ltd
London
Supply plans for Liquid Propane Gas Fired Kiln

Kiln suppliers

Cromartie Kilns Ltd
Park Hall Road Longton Stoke-on-Trent
R. M. Catterson-Smith Ltd
Adam Bridge Works South Way Exhibition Grounds Wembley
Middx
Kilns and Furnaces Ltd
Keele Street Works Tunstall Stoke-on-Trent

Books for Further Study

Michael Cardew, *Pioneer Pottery*, Longmans, 1969
A marvellously comprehensive account of the discovery and use of raw materials from an author with forty-five years' experience as a potter.
Emmanuel Cooper, *A Handbook of Pottery*, Longman, 1970
A survey of the teaching of pottery in school with working methods evolved with special regard for children and teachers.
Bernard Leach, *A Potter's Book*, Faber & Faber, 1945
The first modern book on pottery whch has never been equalled. Bernard Leach is the founder and master of the modern studio pottery movement and the book details his experience.
MAGAZINE: *Ceramic Review*
          5 Belsize Lane, London NW3 5AD
Six issues a year – £2
A complete survey of modern pottery.

Glossary of Terms

Bone China	English type of porcelain fired to around 1150°C made by the pottery industry
Cones	Manufactured pyramids composed of raw materials: used in kilns to denote temperature
Earthenware	Glazed pottery fired to around 1100°C
Extruded	Shapes made by forcing clay through a template
Frit	A melted mixture of raw materials ground into a powder: used mainly for making glazes
Glaze	Type of glass used on pottery to give a smooth waterproof covering which can be made in a variety of colours
Grog	Fired clay which is broken up into a coarse gritty powder and added to clay to reduce shrinkage and give strength
Hydrometer	Simple instrument for measuring glaze or slip density
Kiln	A construction in which clay is heated to bring about changes which turn it into pottery
Kneading	Technique of mixing clay to remove air bubbles and make it more plastic

Luting	Process of joining different parts of a pot together
Metal Oxides	Industrially prepared materials used in pottery to give colour in glazes and slips
Mould	Any sort of former used for making pottery
Plaster of Paris	A prepared form of calcium which, when mixed with water, sets hard to form a porous white absorbent material
Plasticity	Ability of clay to be moulded and modelled
Porcelain	Fine, white, translucent ware usually fired to a high temperature
Pyrometer	Instrument which shows temperature inside the kiln
Reclaim	Clay which, after being used once, is prepared for use again
Refractory	Able to withstand high temperature.
Slurry	Clay mixed with water to form an uneven formless liquid
Stoneware	Hard, non-porous pottery fired to a temperature of around 1250°C
Throwing	Technique of making pots on a fastly spinning wheel by using centrifugal force
Wedging	Process of making clay homogenous by banging, cutting it in half and banging it together.
Viscous	Ability of glazes to remain stationary when soft
Vitrify	To become glass-like and non-porous usually at high temperatures

Index